DON'T CRY DARLIN'

DON'T CRY DARLIN'

Pepper Ritter

Order this book online at www.trafford.com
or email orders@trafford.com

Most Trafford titles are also available at major online book retailers.

Printed in the United States of America.

ISBN: 978-1-4269-7013-9 (sc)
ISBN: 978-1-4269-7014-6 (e)

Library of Congress Control Number: 2011907889

Trafford rev. 08/30/2011

 www.trafford.com

North America & International
toll-free: 1 888 232 4444 (USA & Canada)
phone: 250 383 6864 ♦ fax: 812 355 4082

GOD BLESS THE READER

God Bless the Reader of my writing. I pray that as you read you will experience moments that cause your heart to sing, you will chuckle, your eyes will leak, your face will smile, and you will be unable to control your laughter. I pray you will be lifted so high that your light will be contagious. I pray you are excited to know, without a doubt, that miracles happen. I pray you have enough strength to shed your fears, and the courage to continue forward with positive thoughts, so that you will think and do good things. I pray that you know your memories are educational stepping stones to your future. Most of all, I pray you will be comforted knowing, deep within your soul, there is no measure large enough to express how very much you are loved.

I thank our Heavenly Father for making this book possible, and I appreciate the encouragement He gave me to write about this special time in my life.

And to you, Elvis/Jon/Jesse, I believe our Heavenly Father had a reason for us to meet that one early morning in the Safeway Store. It was a blessing to me, and perhaps it was a blessing for you in a way that is unknown to me. I hope by now you won't be hurt by my taking our chapter from my autobiography, *'What I Remember Before I Forget,'* to write, *'Don't Cry Darlin.'* Perhaps I shouldn't have remembered; but I did. Thank you for spending so much of your time with me. I'm sorry I handled our meeting so poorly. I hope you have few regrets, and that you have exceeded all of your expectations for this life. Perhaps we'll meet again in the next.

ACKNOWLEDGMENTS

To every Elvis fan and reader of this book: We have all been blessed to have a memory of this incredible man. He made us all better by sharing his talent, his kindness, and his love. There is no doubt in my mind that he was given a special calling, and he went above and beyond what was expected of him.

Linda Hood (Shuma) Sigmon, you are a sweet spirit. It hasn't been easy for you to share your many years of friendship with Elvis/Jesse due to the abuse you have been subjected to by fans who don't accept that Elvis simply changed his life-style August 16, 1977. It has to be extremely difficult for you to receive verbal attacks simply because they think you are lying about your friendship with him. It has taken a very strong lady to continue to share him with us. I am grateful that I was led to you, and I am proud and happy to have you for a friend. I welcome anyone to read your wonderful website; lindahoodsigmontruth.com.

My sister, Barb, for replacing my office word 2007 with 2003, in an effort to keep me from having a nervous breakdown.

My #1 granddaughter, Tarah, thanks for being my computer tech so that I could continue writing.

Mark Advent, Author Learning Center Consultant. Your encouragement and words of faith were given when I needed it most. Thank you for getting me back on the right path.

Gail Giorgio, thank you so very much for writing, 'Is Elvis Alive?'.... 'The Elvis Files'....and 'Elvis Undercover-Is He Alive and Coming Back?' And thanks for sharing the tapes. Sharing your interest in Elvis has been a blessing for me and his fans.

My dear friend, Helen Knight, thanks for editing my work.

Robert W. Dye, Elvis Presley Enterprises, Inc., Photography Manager. Your permission to include pictures of Elvis is sincerely appreciated.

Andrew W. Mayoras, Co-Author of Trial & Heirs (www. TrialAndHeirs.com) for making it possible for Shuma to contact me.

Relot-Fre Toler, Make-up Artist, Belk's Lancome skincare, Huntsville, AL. thanks for working miracles and for your well wishes.

Sarah Conner, Portrait Innovations, Huntsville, AL. You worked miracles on my cover portrait.

CONTENTS

One

Who is Elvis Presley?

When Julie called to invite me for dinner and to watch Elvis Presley on the Milton Berle Show, I asked, "Who is Elvis Presley?" I was surprised at her enthusiasm, and told her Milton Berle wasn't one of my favorite people, so I didn't watch his shows.

She nearly damaged my ear drum. "Oh Pepper! You just have to come over and watch Elvis with me. In fact, if you have to ask who he is you are in for a treat, and I don't want you to miss it."

Her excitement was infectious, so I laughingly told her I would be happy to accept her invitation, and I would see her after work the following Tuesday evening. It was a warm June evening in 1956. I had lived in Dallas, 'Big D' as we called it then, for about a year.

Julie was giddy when I arrived. We ate dinner and waited for this new found talent, a twenty-one year old young man from Memphis, Tennessee. He was absolutely amazing. The audience was blown away. Girls were screaming as he sang and gyrated. And I must admit Julie and I screamed while still trying to hear him sing. Julie's brother, Bunk, enjoyed his performance as much as we did. When Elvis sang his last song we wanted to hear more, but he didn't return to the microphone. Julie smiled and said, "Now you know who Elvis Presley is." I thanked her for the invite and went home.

The next day several employees talked about Elvis's performance, and already he was being chastised by some for his movement on stage. I wasn't offended by it, and said that I didn't think he did anything that was considered, 'in poor taste.'

About four months later Julie called again. The excitement in her voice made me eager to hear what she had to say. Elvis was scheduled to perform in the Cotton Bowl, October 11, 1956. She was sure I would want to go. I excitedly told her I did. It was great looking forward to seeing him perform in the city, but the wait was difficult.

It was a warm Thursday night. The stage was in the middle of the football field, and the crowd was humongous. Elvis entered the stadium with an entourage. He sat with his feet on the front seat of a pretty red convertible. The crowd went wild. It's likely there was more noise in the Cotton Bowl that night than there was at any football game played there. I don't remember the price of the ticket, but it was worth every cent.

Elvis had greatness from the very beginning of his career. He had class and a boyish personality. He had sex appeal, but more than that he had a unique voice. I didn't want the night to end. He left the stadium just as he had entered. There was so much shouting for him to return it was almost deafening.

We thought about going to the hotel where he was staying, but then we laughed about how silly we were acting. We figured there would be scads of other hopefuls thinking the same thing, and none of them would be allowed to see him. So we went home, and dreamed about seeing him in person another time. It was a great memory that I have thought about many times.

I moved to Denver in 1958; 'Little D' as we fondly called it. Nearly four years later I returned to Manhattan, Kansas with my daughter, Jami Lynn. She was not quite two years old.

Sometime in April 1977, a friend told me Elvis was on tour and would be in Missouri and Nebraska sometime in June. We were disappointed he didn't have Kansas in his schedule. Kansas City was only a two hour drive, so we could take off work a little early and would be home around one in the morning. I called for tickets and was told the concert was sold out. Lincoln. Nebraska was a two and a half hour drive, but I was told they were sold out too. We crossed our fingers when we asked for tickets to the Omaha concert. It was farther and would take us about three and a half hours, but we so wanted to be in the crowd; and I don't like crowds. In any case, I was again told it was sold out. We were terribly disappointed. I wondered how so many people heard about it before we did. I guess I was just too busy being a mama and an employee. I have since learned the shows in Nebraska were not sold out.

He performed at the Market Square Arena in Indianapolis, Indiana, June 26, 1977. I was disappointed that it wasn't televised; at least it wasn't in my little city.

August 13, 1977 we celebrated Jami's seventeenth birthday. Three days later, Bernie, the United Parcel Service driver, came in with the shocking news that Elvis was dead. It was a terrible Tuesday. Little work was done that afternoon because the employees didn't quit talking about Elvis. I was glad that in less than two hours I could go home and ponder the news.

My boss came into my office and loudly said, laughing, "Someone in Vegas is taking bets that Elvis is alive." He went on to say the man would pay a million dollars to the person who could prove him right. I don't remember the Vegas man's name, but I remember saying, "Perhaps he knows something we don't." And the minute I said it I felt very peaceful. I too had a feeling Elvis was still on this earth. Eventually, time would reveal the truth.

I wished that I had more of his music, but I didn't rush out and buy any. I seldom had extra cash to use for things other than essentials. However, whenever I heard his voice, and saw him on the television I was happy. It was clear from the beginning he was a star; a special spirit put on this earth for a special purpose, and I am sure he accomplished that purpose. His stage presence was genuine, and he always gave so much to his fans.

I recall thinking of a performance I saw on television. He was trying to sing, but there was so much screaming and shouting that it appeared he knew he couldn't be heard, so he stopped singing and barely moved his body, and the audience increased their roaring noise. After doing this a few times, it appeared Elvis thought it funny, but at the same time his facial expression said, 'Why am I doing this? All I have to do is move my little finger and they applaud.' But it was his impish personality and extraordinary talent whom we loved. It seemed like we just couldn't get enough. And the more he gave, the more we expected.

And now it was reported he had died of an apparent heart attack. I couldn't wrap my brain around the fact that he was actually gone from this earth. It wasn't because I didn't want him to be dead. It was more than that. I simply had a strong feeling that he had not died. I kept thinking, 'why? Why did you do it this way?'

I thought about his concert tour, and how disappointed the thousands of ticket holders would be. He was scheduled to perform in Portland, Maine, August 17 and 18. Shows were scheduled in eight more cities, and the tour was to end in Memphis August 27 and 28. He had a grueling schedule. In five months he had fifty-eight shows in fifty cities. It seems to me that is pushing the body to its limits. And it wasn't just Elvis; it was the band members, the singers' and whoever else was needed to put on such great concerts. They all had a grueling schedule. Now, however, I imagine all those engaged in working with Elvis have great memories of those days.

About two months after Elvis's reported death, his last concert was going to be televised. I was just as excited and anxious to watch it as Julie had been in 1955 when she called to invite me to watch him perform on the Milton Berle show. It was a great show. His voice was strong. He was in control as he belted out the words, 'you won't forget me when I go.' And when he sang 'Hurt' I got goose bumps. It was as if this song had personal meaning to him. I was so happy to hear him sing, 'Bridge Over Trouble Waters' once again. He was magnificent. I have never heard anyone sing this song as well. The words, 'When you're down and out' and 'and pain is all around' were sang with such feeling that my eyes leaked. And this time when he sang, 'It's now or never,' I knew it was. I was so not ready for him to begin, 'Can't help falling in love', because I just didn't want the moment to end.

He made so many introductions my head was spinning, and it seemed like he gave out more scarfs than he had at other performances I had seen. He stayed on stage longer than I had seen him do in the past. He actually seemed to enjoy shaking hands. He thrived on all the love the crowd was showering on him. It appeared he was having fun.

Before he left the stage I felt ill. I felt like my heart was on a trampoline. It was clear to me; he was saying goodbye. He was telling us this was his last stage performance. I remembered him saying, 'Till we meet you again, may God bless you. Adios' or something similar. He was telling us a big change was coming to all of us, but he wasn't actually saying the words. And once again I asked, 'Why? Why did you do it this way? I didn't know then that one day I would receive an answer.

Two

Don't Cry Darlin'

Before I continue I want to bear my testimony that my words are true. I would not manufacture such a story. This special happening in my life has caused much stress for me. I'm not sure why it has affected me in a stressful way, but I believe it's because of the shock it caused. In any case, Heavenly Father is my witness to the truth of my words.

Two years before it was announced that Elvis had died I made a very bad decision. After a very short courtship I was in love. I was thirty-seven, and bursting with happiness. My daughter, Jami, was twelve years old, and would have her heart's desire; a daddy. In less than a year I was in an abusive marriage. My husband had a dark side; a very mean heart. Finally in 1986, I said, "Enough is enough." I needed to put distance between my husband and me. Jami was married with three children, and had recently moved to Germany. My mama lived in a nursing home in Anchorage, Alaska, and so on Jami's twenty-sixth birthday I flew Delta to Anchorage. I thought three weeks would be enough time to think things through, and see some of the beautiful state with mama. The three weeks turned into twenty-one wonderful years.

Sometime in early 1987 I began supplementing my day job with a weekend, nighttime, child care position. I worked for a twenty-four-seven child care facility near my home. It was a fun job. Occasionally I worked an extra shift, but it was a bit tiring because I worked until midnight or three in the morning.

The Safeway store was on the corner of Northern Lights Blvd and Boniface Parkway where I turned to go home. After several nights, I became curious why there were always three cars parked at the entrance, to the back side, of the store. It seemed a bit unusual to pick that as a place to congregate. Some nights a few guys were standing beside the cars. It appeared like they were blocking the way to get behind the building. I wondered why they didn't simply park in the section designated for parking. There were seldom any cars in the parking lot at that hour.

Early one morning, I turned the corner before I remembered I intended to stop at the store, so I turned into the drive at the back of the building where the three cars were parked. There were several guys standing outside, just laughing and talking. Again, I wondered why they congregated there instead of a restaurant parking lot, or one of the department store parking lots. I thought it was strange they parked so they would have to move if delivery trucks arrived. Maybe they knew delivery trucks entered at the east side of the building, or maybe they knew the delivery schedule. In any case, I rushed in to buy a loaf of specialty bread. When I left the cars were still there when I drove by.

I took two weeks off from my night work. When I returned I noticed the cars were not parked by the back entrance of the store. After a few weeks I didn't notice. I'm not sure why, but I just didn't look in that direction. Perhaps it was because I was tired and perhaps it was because I worked later than usual.

Early in the morning of March 12, 1988, I stopped at Safeway's for another loaf of specialty bread. It was about three-fifteen. I entered from the front side of the store. Again no cars were in the lot, but the three cars were blocking the west entrance to the back of the store. I rushed in and glanced to the checkout counters to the right. There was one clerk on duty. He was talking to a guy who I thought must be an employee or perhaps from one of the cars parked at the back side of the store.

The kind of bread I wanted was sold out, so I simply turned to leave. As I turned to walk down an aisle towards the door the guy, who had been at the checkout, was turning into the same aisle at the opposite end.

It was strange that we picked the same aisle. If either of us had turned on a different aisle I would have missed being a part of a miracle, or if I had shopped for anything else I would not be writing this book.

I have a habit, good or bad; I don't know which, of speaking to everyone. I've always thought some people need someone to acknowledge them or give them a smile. In any case, it can't hurt anyone. This was no exception. I was ready to make a comment, even if it was a simple, "Hello," but as I got a few steps from him he quickly turned and reached for a can on the top shelf, so I had no eye contact with him. I didn't take my eyes off him because I still intended to speak to him. He never turned, so I continued on. He just stood there touching the can like he was going to pick it up. About five steps past him I came to a screeching halt. I just couldn't ignore what I thought I saw. Since I had already passed him I'm surprised that he didn't high tail it out the back.

I turned around and walked slowly until I had passed him. I stopped and turned around to look at him. He was still touching the same can, and it looked like he was looking out the corner of his eye to see what I was doing. Once again; I walked a few steps past him, stopped, and turned again, and just stared at him. It looked like he was stuck in that position. I walked past him again. I pondered whether I should just forget it and go on home. However, I just couldn't forget about it, so I walked past him again; he still hadn't moved.

It's not my nature to be so bold, but finally I walked towards him, and said, "Excuse me; you look like, Elvis Presley." He didn't move. He pretended not to hear me. So I moved a couple of steps closer. Speaking louder, I said, "Excuse me, you look like, Elvis Presley." This time he turned to look at me. He smiled, but said nothing. By then, I was standing right beside him, and I nearly screamed, "Wow! You really look like Elvis."

He looked directly into my eyes, smiled, stood for a moment, and then he grinned, and said, "If you don't tell anybody, I won't." And let me tell you my knees turned to mush. I didn't faint; however, I thought I was going to. I wondered if the color had drained from my face.

There was no way to control what happened next. I actually fell into him, so that he had to hold me up; and I cried. It amazed me that I could manufacture so many tears in just a moment. As I held on tight I squeezed his flesh. In fact, I was squeezing and releasing my grip, and then squeezed some more. It seemed like I was actually kneading his flesh. It is amazing that I still remember exactly what he felt like. Feeling his flesh brought me back to reality, because I knew I wasn't dreaming.

It didn't matter what he looked like or who he looked like, but the fact is; he looked like Elvis. He apparently didn't think it was necessary to use a disguise after so many years, but regardless, there was one thing he could never disguise, and that is his voice. It was Elvis. And he was trimmed down to the way he was before he put on all the weight. He looked great, I could feel a teensy bit of excess flesh around his waist line, but with clothes on it was not the least bit noticeable.

I was surprised that he wasn't wearing a hat. For some reason I thought he would be. I was surprised that he wasn't wearing sunglasses; even though it was the wee hours of the morning. I'm confident he never expected meeting anyone. He wore blue jeans and an unbuttoned blue denim jacket over a white shirt with the first few buttons unbuttoned. He didn't have any grey hair, so I imagine he has dyed it, but he looked absolutely fantastic. His hair was thick and shiny, and he had the curl over the 'right' side of his forehead.

He didn't have long thick sideburns, but he had sideburns that were trimmed close to his face, and they reached just to the top of his lower ear lobes. I was surprised, he didn't have a mustache or beard since it might have given him a look that wasn't as noticeable; many men in Alaska have facial hair. I thought if he was trying to disguise his identity it would be perfect for him, but he apparently didn't think it was necessary, or he simply didn't like facial hair. I was glad he didn't.

I was embarrassed by my actions, and I wasted precious time. Instead of talking to him, I had my head buried in his chest, and my fingers were kneading his back. I was actually hugging Elvis Presley, and he was hugging me, but only out of concern for me.

He said, "Don't cry darlin'." I was so in shock I couldn't push myself away from him. We were both standing with our arms around each other, and suddenly I realized I must be putting him in an extremely uncomfortable situation. Next I wondered how I could make this situation easier on him. He said, "Please don't cry." But I continued to sob. They were happy tears, and they were tears caused from shock; and I was totally shocked.

After quite a while I finally quit crying; then I looked up at him. I didn't realize he was so tall. I'm five-foot-two, and I had to look way up at him. When I've seen him perform on TV, he doesn't look tall to me. In any case, he took a hold of my shoulders and looked down. Our eyes met, and he asked, "Are you okay?"

Then I did a really stupid thing because I wanted him to feel safe. Like I said, I was still in shock. Talk about stupid; I answered his question by saying, "You're not Elvis."

He said, "I'm not? Why would you say that?"

I blurted out, "Because Elvis doesn't have blue eyes."

He grinned, and said, "I don't?"

I continued to make stupid comments. I told him, 'Elvis has brown eyes."

He continued to grin, and said, "I do?"

I said that because I really thought he was wearing contacts because his eyes are brown in the poster size picture I have of him. I told him I didn't have all of his records, and I hadn't seen all of his movies. I didn't mention the reason for that is because I never had enough funds to buy them, and I still don't, but one day I would love to have a complete collection of everything he has done, and I mean beyond August 1977.

I told him I felt bad that Elvis had gained weight because it wasn't healthy. Gads! Now I have many unwanted pounds. I told him I never believed the overdose story or that he used the amount of drugs that was reported. I told him when I heard of his death I had a gut feeling that he was still alive, and I couldn't understand why I felt so strong about it; but I was sure it was more than wishful thinking. I told him when I heard stories that he had been seen; I was confident he was actually still alive.

I had wondered for a long time why he would fake his death, and I told him I could imagine how he felt to have scads of people screaming and grabbing at him, and he must have seldom had any peace. Then I added that I just loved him. I told him I was shocked at meeting him, but I wouldn't tell anyone.

He laughed and said, "It's okay if you do. No one would believe you anyway." He laughed again.

I imagine that was a correct statement. And then I shut up. I mean I couldn't talk. My heart was pounding so hard I thought he might hear it.

Then he started talking to me. I know he talked about the drugs, his weight, why he faked his death, but I only heard words; not full sentences. I was in a daze while he was talking. My eyes were blurry as I looked at him. It seemed like a curtain of gauze shielded them. We were still touching all the time he talked to me. I couldn't tell you how many times he asked me if I was alright. He truly showed a genuine concern for me; which was overwhelming. He really is a southern gentleman.

And I must say, Heavenly Father sure put him together nice. He was fifty-three and still a 'hunk.' But even though I say this, I didn't have a 'crush' on him. But I would have been thrilled to be his sister and loyal friend.

The clerk appeared from the back of the store. He looked at us as he walked towards us very slowly. I was sure he had been talking to Elvis's friends. We moved to the other side of the aisle. We were silent while he walked past us. I couldn't see Elvis's expression because I was in front of him, and we were both facing the clerk. Elvis could have mouthed something to him, and I wouldn't have known.

When he turned at the end of the aisle, Elvis said, "Are you sure you're okay?" I shook my head slowly from side to side. I was embarrassed because we continued to stand so close to each other that we were still touching and neither one of us had said anything for a few minutes. I'm sure we were both in shock.

I imagine every time he was put in this situation it was difficult for him. After all, more and more people knew, without a doubt, he did not die in 1977. And now I was blessed to be one of them.

About ten minutes after the clerk walked back to the front of the store, a woman appeared at the end of the isle at the back of the store. She stood there for a moment, and looked at us with a disgusted expression. She looked familiar. I stood looking at her trying to determine if I might know who she was. She was about my height; perhaps an inch or two taller. Actually, I thought she looked a lot like Priscilla; without makeup. However, I couldn't imagine Priscilla without makeup; even in Alaska. She said impatiently, "Did you get the jalapeno peppers?"

He said, "Yes."

If he had them....they were in his pocket. I almost told him, 'I will always remember what she asked you, because my name is 'Pepper.'

Then she said, with a frown, "Are you coming?" He told her he would be there in a minute. She turned around and walked out of sight.

Then he asked me, "Are you sure you are okay?" I told him, I would be.

He said, "I'm sorry, but I really have to go." I told him I understood, and he walked away.

As he walked slowly to the back of the store I walked towards the checkout. Something told me to turn around. He was still walking slowly. I yelled, "Excuse me." He stopped, and turned around with a smile on his face.

I said, "What name do you use now?"

He answered, "John Barrows"

I smiled and said, "Thanks, and God bless you John Barrows. Have a good life."

He smiled, nodded, turned to continue walking, and raised his left arm with a quick wave. Then he looked down. I watched him until he was out of sight.

When I got to the checkout the clerk was standing there looking a bit nervous. I smiled, and said, "Wow, I'm still in shock."

"You are?"

"Yeh! You have quite a celebrity in your store,"

He looked at me sheepishly and said, "Who?"

"You know who."

"Tell me."

"No, I don't think he would want me to tell anyone, so I might as well start now."

I told him I had come in for a loaf of specialty bread, and was disappointed because they were sold out. However, it didn't matter, and I hoped I would remember this special night for the rest of my life. And then I told him it was amazing that we chose the same aisle at the same time to walk down, and if I wasn't such a friendly person I would have missed out on a fantastic experience."

I imagine there are people who have actually walked past Elvis, or stood beside him without knowing it.

The clerk told me he would do me a favor. I said, "When you see him will you tell him I'm sorry I acted so stupid, but I was in shock; In fact, I'm still in shock. And please tell him his secret is safe with me."

He smiled, and said, "I'd be happy too." I thanked him.

Then I reached for a pack of gum, and told him, "I want to buy something so I will have a receipt of this day." He laughed and told me to sleep well. I smiled and said, "I doubt that will happen."

When I turned to walk out of the store I saw a penny on the floor; close to the door. I leaned down and picked it up. Just before I got to my car I leaned down to pick up another penny. There was no one to give them to, so I put them in my pocket. It has been a habit of mine ever since I was about eight years of age to give away the pennies I found....even to a total stranger. I had been taught the jingle many of you have heard. 'Find a penny....pick it up....From now on you will have good luck.' But I added these words to the jingle, 'but give it to a friend and you will have double luck.' I was happy to have good luck, but I thought it would be nice to give the luck to someone else, especially if I were going to have double luck. I was always afraid I would forget to give the penny away, because I didn't know when I would see a friend. So right then and there I made the decision a perfect stranger could be my friend. After I picked up pennies I found I simply walked to the first person I saw with my hand held out to them. They in turn reached for my hand, and bless their hearts they stood listening to me speak the words of my jingle. The very first time I did that I was greeted with kind words, thank you, smiles, or some who said they had never heard the last part of my jingle. I was happy to tell them I made it up, because I wanted to give others good luck...and besides, I then would double my luck. And you know what, the moment we spoke, we were no longer strangers....We were friends.

Before I opened my car door the cars that were parked in the back zoomed to the front of the building, and out onto the Parkway. They turned west at the corner onto Northern Lights Boulevard.

I heard a lot of laughter when they drove through the lot. I wondered if they were laughing at me, laughing at Elvis, or laughing at the situation. I hoped they weren't laughing at me.

If I hadn't been so in shock, I would have driven down the boulevard to check out all the restaurants. It was obvious to me, there was a waitress or waiter someplace who knew Elvis was in the city, at least for a while. However, I hadn't heard of any 'sightings.'

I do believe anyone in Alaska, who saw him, protected him. In any case, sometime later, I thought how cool it would have been to walk directly up to him and his friends, and maybe with my camera just to see what would have happened. I drove home instead. My body was trembling with excitement all the way.

It was all I could do not to wake Susie to tell her what happened, but I had made a promise that I would keep 'My sighting' to myself. I felt like screaming with excitement, but I managed to control myself. I put the receipt in my bottom dresser drawer, and then looked at the dates on my new found pennies. It was strange. One of the pennies was dated 1977, the year Elvis was reported to have died, and the other was the present year; 1988.

I quietly went to bed; my mind had a difficult time shutting down. When the music woke me…. I knew I had slept.

The next few days I felt like I was walking on air, and I believe I was still in shock. I had a difficult time staying focused because I just couldn't stop thinking about meeting Elvis. I knew then why I had been prompted for so long to buy a pocket recorder. I have tortured myself many times because I don't use my smarts, or I use them in such a stupid way. I wanted to tell everybody about my time with Elvis, but I kept it to myself. I now think it wasn't good for my mental health.

I wondered if Elvis was waiting to see if I had reported a 'sighting.' And I wondered how he felt after moments like that happened. I felt sorry that he made the decision to 'retire,' but I knew he put a lot of thought into his decision to do so. Anyway I regret wasting time saying nothing instead of having more conversation with him. I wish I would have asked him questions. I wish I had asked if he regretted his actions on August 16, 1977. I think there are times he has.

A few days later, I picked up Susie's newspaper from the table and glanced through it. I seldom read the paper, and never read the personals; but this day I did. I'm not sure why I did, but I read every one of them. One ad said something like, "Would the young lady I met in the supermarket call this number. I think I'd like to get to know you better." For a brief moment I thought someone else had an encounter in a grocery store, not like mine, but someone was trying to locate them. I knew it couldn't be Elvis looking for me because I sure was not a young lady at fifty-three; or was I?

Three

Is Elvis Alive?

About three months after my encounter I drove down the hill to Safeway. Inside the entrance was a book rack filled with a book titled, 'Is Elvis Alive?' Gail Brewer-Giorgio is the author. I smiled and quickly picked up a copy. I was so excited I could hardly wait to read it. It was fascinating to someone who knew the answer to the question. As soon as I put away my groceries I began reading; I couldn't put it down. I thought it strange that it was out so soon after I met him.

A few weeks later I saw the same book; only this edition had a cassette tape attached to the front. So I bought another book. The tape was incredible. How anyone who could believe that it was an imposter talking for Elvis is beyond me. I wondered if the person who recorded the conversations did it hoping to make some money or if they did it because Elvis wanted them to. If Elvis didn't ask for the tape to be 'leaked,' and money was the motive, I imagine he would have been totally disappointed in them for taping his conversations.

Anyone of us can speculate, and we do, but that's just it…speculation. It could very well be that Elvis asked that the information be 'leaked' because he felt guilty that his fans thought he was dead. He wants his fans to know the truth, or as much as he can share with them. I know he wanted to come clean. However, since so many years have passed, I imagine Priscilla and Lisa Marie wouldn't allow him to. And now they wouldn't want the spotlight on them because it would be embarrassing that they had lied.

Graceland was and is making so much money that Priscilla could have thought finding out Elvis was still alive would put the brakes on their financial success. And now at this age I imagine it would be difficult for Elvis to deal with it; unless he has kept himself as young 'in heart' as I have.

About six weeks after I met him, one of my co-workers came into my office, and said, "Pepper, you like Elvis, don't you?" I smiled and said that I did. She suggested that I listen to KYAK, a local radio station, because they played a lot of Elvis, and they talked about him a lot; mostly making fun of him for being fat and using drugs. I started listening. Debra was right; they truly did put Elvis down, which generated several phone calls from listeners that came to his defense, or who criticized the DJ for making such disrespectful comments.

I listened to the station because I enjoyed listening to Elvis sing. The sound of his voice is great mental therapy for me. About six or seven months after my encounter with Elvis I was at my desk when the DJ said, "The first employee to arrive at the station this morning found a large box on the doorstep. It's full of forty-five records of 'Heart Break Hotel.' No one here has any idea who left the box, but we are giving them away to whoever stops by for one." I knew immediately Elvis was responsible for it, but wondered what his reason was.

About an hour later, Debra rushed into my office, and quietly told me before I arrived the DJ had told the listeners' he had the strangest thing happen, and he wanted to share it with them. He said to be sure to stay tuned because he knew the listeners would want to hear it with their own ears, and he announced when he would play it.

I turned my radio up and waited; and he announced it again. I obviously didn't have a clue to what he was going to share with us. When it was time I quit working, and I turned on my pocket recorder that I purchased after my encounter with Elvis. I did listen to the prompting; just not when I should have.

He played a recording of a caller who wanted to know why they were so hard on Elvis. The caller was defending Elvis. In the meantime, the DJ sounded surprised, shocked, and dumbfounded, because the caller sounded exactly like Elvis. The DJ asked the caller to tell him his name, but he didn't. The DJ nervously said something like, "Is this a joke? Man! You have the voice down pat."

The one thing that I was excited about was at some point in the conversation, he said something like, "Whoever brings Elvis in with a dime on their hand will be given a million dollars." I knew that wasn't likely to happen, but it blew my mind that they had made such an offer only because they thought Elvis was dead. I hope to locate that tape, and include the actual conversation in my story. I knew it was Elvis, and anyone who was listening, who knew Elvis was still alive, would know it was Elvis. In addition many people who heard that conversation must have surely pricked up their ears, and seriously wondered.

Yeah! I found the tape. It was Friday, October 14, 1988. I can't understand the last name of the DJ, but I believe his name is Dennis Able. It was eight-thirteen in the morning when he said, "Is Elvis alive or is he dead? 563-4334. I'm personally convinced that Elvis is running around and I think he's here. I think he's right around here somewhere. I mean…. last night two hundred copies….sometime during the night…. of 'Heartbreak Hotel,' the Elvis forty-five was left outside the front office doors here. Now record companies don't normally deliver their complimentary things that way. You know what I mean? They're here. There's been rumors of sightings at Seven Elevens' around the ding dong counters and things like that, and then this morning a little after nine I released the results here of the survey we've been taking, and have a very special interview."

He said around nine he would play the special interview. Then there were several songs played, and current news reported. I kept wondering when, on earth, they were going to let us hear the special interview because it was after nine. Finally, he said, "I have uh…. in about a half hour from now, there about, we'll be playing an interview…. a telephone interview for you…. with me and a very suspicious sounding voice….received early this morning. Now I want to play this for you, and you decide for yourself who you think it is. It'll be about ten minutes after nine."

Debra was listening to her radio, and was also impatient. We were working, but we weren't giving it our all, because we couldn't concentrate. We didn't want to get so busy that we missed it.

Then the DJ said, "In the unofficial voting poll I took three hours previous to this on whether or not you think Elvis is alive, forty-six people think Elvis is indeed alive, now why would forty-six people think he was alive? Fifty-five people think he is dead, so we have a little bit of a majority there, and three people just don't care."

I didn't call in because I couldn't have said, "I think Elvis is alive." I would have had to say, "I know Elvis is alive, or that he was living March 12, 1988."

The DJ continues, "When I came to work this morning we found two hundred singles of Heartbreak Hotel outside by our door….in the dark….in a box. If you want a copy of the mysterious 'Heartbreak Hotel' swing by our office, and pick up a copy. Since deliveries aren't usually made like that I got suspicious, and then I got this phone call."

DJ, "KYAK"
Caller, "Hello"
DJ, "Hello"
Caller, "Hello"
DJ, "Who is this?"

Caller, "Just call me, (inaudible) Sideburns."

DJ, "I can't hear you." The reason he said this is because it wasn't clear what was said except, 'Sideburns.'

Caller, "Is this KYAK?"

DJ, "Your voice sounds familiar to me."

Caller, "Oh no, it doesn't."

DJ, "Yes this is KYAK. What can I do for you?"

Caller, "I was kind of upset about this whole.... this Elvis thing....because of what you're doin'. I just wish you would let me, I just wish you would let Elvis....Elvis die. The man is dead. He's been gone."

DJ, "You.... Huh! Are you sure I don't know you?"

Caller, "No... I'm sure. I don't even know who you are Dennis."

DJ, "Are you calling from town here?"

Caller, "Uh, yes, I'm a.... I'm a faithful listener to KYAK."

DJ, "You wouldn't happen to have anything to do with these two hundred albums that we got out here at the station, would you?"

Caller: "I don't know anything about those two hundred albums of Heartbreak Hotel that someone left on your doorstep."

DJ, "How did you know it was Heartbreak Hotel?"

Caller, "Well, didn't you say that?"

DJ, "No, You said that."

Caller, "I don't know. I just figured if somebody was going to leave an album that was a good album of Elvis. He did that very well."

DJ, "Oh I don't know. I thought he did better."

Caller, "How about 'Suspicious Minds'? That's always been one of my favorites. Could I maybe request that?"

DJ, "You uh....you want to request it.? Are you sure I don't know you? Your voice sounds so"

Caller, "I had some dental work done the other day, and my mouth is kinda....listen buddy, I gotta.... I really gotta go. Okay? Suspicious minds would make me really happy this morning."

DJ, "Suspicious Minds'?"

Caller, "Suspicious Minds...Yeah."

DJ, "Okay, but I sure wish you would hang around for a minute. I...."

Caller, "No.... No.... I gotta go man."

DJ, "Well... Okay."

Caller, "Thank you, thank you very much, very much."

DJ, "Bye."

It would have been fun to see the expression on Dennis's face. Since early in the conversation he was really getting excited.

Then Dennis said, "Well, there you have it." And he repeated the survey results, and said, "I'll leave it to you to make up your mind." 'Suspicious Minds,' was played. After the song was over Dennis said, "I prefer to believe he is alive, and he's out there somewhere, maybe in the bush, maybe walking along in his bunny boots getting in shape."

I laughed and thought, 'If he only knew.'

My tape continues; I forgot to turn it off. Now I'm on the phone with an Anchorage customer, who had heard the interview; he was excited about it too. It amazes me that Elvis is loved by men and women alike....and all ages. That's a pretty good testimony of how much people enjoy his talent.

Our conversation starts with me saying, "You know.... you know.... I think it's so sad, really.... I mean if.... if you did find him.... and you're putting all that on TV. You know the last thing he wants....you know I just think.... you know.... this man has gone through so much to give up all that he gave up for the reasons that he did what he did.... and then years later.... people are still....."

"And I'm sure he had no idea it would go this far. But to never be able to live a normal life because people still love him and would want to...."

"Yeh! And.... you know.... it would be marvelous if the gentleman could walk down the street and just have people say, "Hi Elvis, how you doin?" You know…. like you might somebody else. But to end up with a mob who each want to take a piece of him with them. That is sad….such a sad thing…."

"Yeh! Will I'm gonna watch and I just….well I know it's newsy….and I just…."

"Well….at least he's here and safe for now. I know that not everyone in the 'lower-forty-eight' can come up here real easy." We laughed and ended our conversation. I began working, but I kept the radio on.

Gads! I used to have a terrible bad habit of saying, 'You know.' I broke myself from saying it, and it certainly wasn't easy….but I did it. I wish I would have been able to record what the customer said.

The station was bombarded with many calls. I wish they had repeated the three hour survey. Without a doubt, I'm convinced the outcome would have been quite different. It was clearly Elvis. Like I said before, no one could sound exactly like Elvis….and especially for so long.

That night I turned on my radio, and tuned to KYAK. In a very short time the DJ said, "Believe it or not….some people think Elvis Presley is hiding out right here in Alaska. Tonight we have this exclusive report on the elusive Elvis." This DJ was easy to understand, and I learned the morning DJ's name is J. Dennis Evans; not Able as I said earlier. And he repeated the story about the box of 'Heartbreak Hotel' forty-fives.

This time the sound was totally clear. Perhaps there was some interference inside DHL. He said, "The man said his name was Billie Bob Sidebricks." I don't know where on earth he got the 'Sidebricks,' because it was clear he said, 'Sideburns'….very clear.

It didn't take long for the DJ to begin making fun of Elvis…. "But it was the anonymous tip that clinched it. We've had some reports of him being in a Laundromat. Uh, there's even some folks saying he lives across the street in the mobile homes over there. It was all starting to add up. We knew we were on to something. We went up the stairs and turned off the lights. We had just settled in for the stake out, but suddenly we were blinded by the flash of sequins. It was almost as if he knew we were watching him."

Then a female's voice yelled, "Elvis."

The DJ continued, "It was so close....but he got away." Next they were playing, 'Caught in a trap.'

The DJ continues, "We aren't giving up. Over at Eagle 97 the DJ's there have set up a fool proof Elvis trap. They've set out this giant jelly donut to lure Elvis in; when he goes for it the net will drop. These guys aren't about to take any chances either. They've even got a backup."

Then another guy says, "My job is the official Elvis trap keeper. If the net malfunctions then my job is to go and trap him with this large net right here as he waddles out of the studio."

The DJ continues, "The Eagle crew isn't just waiting for Elvis to take the bait; they've scraped together a one million dollar bounty. Every nickel is yours if you drop a dime on the King, and bring him in."

Then the guy from Eagle 97 says, "Let's get it cleared up. Come on....there's been lot's of fooling around, but we want the real Elvis Presley to just come clean. Come on Elvis."

And then the KYAK DJ says, "And remember; you saw him here first."

After listening to the tape, I can see I didn't remember it exactly right, but I was close, and that makes me happy to know my mind is still pretty good even though it sometimes is fuzzy when my brain gets scrambled. I remembered nothing about Eagle 97. I thought it was KYAK who made the statement about the million dollars. Maybe they both made the offer.

I believe even now if Elvis would walk in there with anyone and a dime, they would have to pay out the million dollars.

That's not likely to happen though, and if they did I imagine Eagle 97 or KYAK would deny the statement had ever been made, and that's when my tape would be helpful. Life is so fun, and yet after hugging Elvis it has also been undeniably mind-boggling.

Many times, since meeting him in Safeway's, I have mentally beaten myself up because I didn't listen to the prompting. For several months that little voice inside me told me to get a camera and a tape recorder, and the little voice even told me the type of recorder. It was a pocket recorder that would automatically record when it heard voices when it was set in that mode. I kept hearing the prompting, but because I didn't understand why I should do it....I didn't act on it. If I would have had it with me that morning, and I wasn't acting so weird when we met, I could have turned it on, and asked him if I could have the clerk take a picture of us together. He might have allowed it. At least I would have been prepared. And later when I thought he had really gone on to bigger and better things I could have sold the tape for more than a million. I could have done so much good with the money.

I totally handled an opportunity of a lifetime so poorly, simply because I was concerned about another person's feelings; and that person was Elvis Presley. Gads! Thinking back on it, I'm certain he could have and would have handled whatever I did or said like a gentleman.

It has been a long time since I have heard about any 'sightings,' so maybe he is gone now. But I figure if there has ever been a time that Graceland was temporarily shut down, that would be to put Elvis in his casket and remove the wax model. However, maybe the plan isn't to bury him there. Maybe he wants to be cremated like I do. Actually, we don't know for a fact if his Grandma, Mama and Daddy are buried at Graceland.

Through the years there has been talk of exhuming the body in the casket, but I am confident that no one would give permission....because the wax figure would still be the wax figure. Even after his real burial, no one would ever give permission because it would be clear that he hadn't died in 1977.

So many times I wish I would have kept a journal so that I could write the exact dates of when what happened, but I imagine I would have a difficult time locating all the journals, so it makes little difference. So now I just have to guess about the duration of time.

I believe Elvis's fans would be thrilled to know he is still alive, but just like me; they would most likely have been disappointed in him at first because he took his music away from us. However, once he explained why he did what he did, people would understand; just as I do. He definitely has reasons' for doing what he did.

He could have continued to make albums so we could continue to enjoy his talent. And he could have stayed in the background so he wouldn't have to deal with so many out of control crowds. Perhaps he did, but many of us wouldn't have heard his music, so we wouldn't have been able to buy it. It's easy to speculate. I imagine Elvis has many times.

I read that Barbra Streisand quit performing on stage because crowds make her nervous. Even when she couldn't handle the stress she continued to share her talent by making albums for her fans. If Elvis had someone to convince him to continue making recordings, and simply make an announcement that he was no longer going to perform on stage or on tour, people would have been disappointed and disgruntled, but they would have accepted it. However, I imagine there would be many who wouldn't have allowed him to have his privacy.

On the other hand, if people would think back to the events that were taking place prior to August 16, 1977, they would realize he may very well have found a way out of the limelight so people would think he was dead. I imagine he thought it was the only way to keep his family and himself safe. Perhaps he was right. In any case, I'm glad we didn't have to find out.

It would have been hard for him to make such a difficult decision. None of us knows what we would do in the same position; unless we were actually in the position. Remember the saying about walking in someone else's shoes. It really is so true.

Years ago when he still needed the general public to know he had died he made phone calls to someone who recorded his conversations. Some people believe he was talking to a male cousin; others think it was a good friend. It is not known if he asked that his conversations be taped to use in the future. In any case, sometime in 1987 or 1988 Gail Brewer-Giorgio, author of, 'Is Elvis Alive,' was given a tape of these conversations to use as she wanted to. They had read her book, 'Orion,' and knew the book was pulled from shelves all over the country before it could be purchased. They thought this treatment was unfair, and I imagine they didn't want the same thing to happen to her new book, "Is Elvis Alive;' they wanted her to know everything she had written in her book was true. All voices had purposely been deleted except Elvis's. It is obvious he is talking to someone; answering their questions as well as having a normal conversation with them. And since this was the compilation of more than one conversation, he sometimes repeats his concerns. The tape was authenticated to be the voice of Elvis Presley.

Elvis tells us he has recorded since August 16, 1977. If I had the finances I would do some research and hope to locate the albums. Obviously he couldn't use the name of Elvis Presley, but what name did he use? If anyone has this knowledge I wish they would share it with me.

When I purchased the book, that included the tape, I read, 'Mystery tape....believed to have been recorded around 1981.' The first recording could have been in 1981, however I thought Gail was given the wrong year because they didn't want her to know it was so recent. After reading the book about the fifth time I finally noticed the date of the voice authentication was a few months before our encounter.

It's easy to speculate. We continue to say, perhaps or maybe, however, one thing I know is this: Elvis has certainly kept us guessing. It's clear to me, he has purposely caused the confusion, and I'm sure it has made him chuckle many times.

Gail left contact information in her book, so I hoped she would return my call. I wanted permission to use the tape in my book because I know, after twenty-three years, there are many who did not have the opportunity to read her book, and listen to the tape. I know you would enjoy it. She called and informed me that Legend Books owns the copyrights of the tape, and they went out of business in 1999 or the early part of 2000. Tudor Publishing owns the rights to the book, and they went out of business many years ago. Since she doesn't own the rights to the book she can't give me permission to include the content of the tape in my book. It's disappointing. It seems to me there should be a way to use it under these circumstances, but I don't have the energy or the time to make it through all the copyright laws. I have already spent many hours on it, and it is absolutely mindboggling. I certainly recommend that you read these books: 'Is Elvis Alive?'.... 'The Elvis Files,' that was published in 1994, by Shapolsky Publishers, Inc. and 'Elvis Undercover-Is He Alive and Coming Back?' 'Elvis Undercover,'was published in 1999, by Tudor Publishing. It is difficult to find them since they are out of print, but with a little effort you will succeed, and then if you want to sell them back for someone else to enjoy you can. I couldn't part with mine, and I have read them all several times. Perhaps one day she will do another printing.

Another thing to help you is that you can search on the internet for the interview of the tape. I found it. The interview is being conducted by Legend Books with Gail, the author of the novel 'Orion' and a book about the book, entitled, 'The Most Incredible Elvis Presley Story Ever Told.' I will save you a lot of time because I imagine, after hearing the tape, you will want to read the book that is mentioned. I looked for months, and couldn't find it. Finally, I learned the title had been changed to, 'Is Elvis Alive?'

I have read, 'Orion.' It is a fun read. You won't want to put it down; that is if you can find it. I happened across it when it was first published in February, 1989, by Tudor Publishing Company. And I must say I marvel at how well Gail can put a book together in such an intriguing and interesting way.

The first time I read that Jon Burrows was one of the names Elvis used I nearly fainted. I heard him wrong when we met, but I was certainly close. I didn't think of how he spelled his name. And Barrows and Burrows; well don't fault me. I wish I had asked him what his middle name is; somehow I have a feeling its 'Presley.'

Some years back…way back…long before my encounter with Elvis, I heard that people were still writing letters to him. So apparently he was given the mail that was sent. I thought about writing, but I thought it would go into a 'dead letter file.' No pun intended. It's almost unbelievable that I had the opportunity to tell him how I felt about him long before our encounter. If there's anything super-natural about Elvis Presley, it is his talent.

The first time I read that Elvis referred to women as 'young ladies' I felt faint. It occurred to me that perhaps his upbringing and his southern gentleman ways would cause him to describe a fifty-three year old woman as a 'young lady.' He is three months and nine days younger than I am, so I'm confident we knew each other prior to coming down.

When we met there was absolutely no sign of drugs. His eyes were very clear. In fact, he appeared to be in perfect health without any evidence of previous drug use. He looked no different than any of us would look while we were using prescription drugs. That makes me think he played his part in making people think he was into the drug scene in order to do what he hoped to do. In my opinion, he knew it would hurt his image, but he had to make a choice. However, I don't think he had a clue what would be written about him or how much it would hurt him. The tabloids were doing a great business at his expense. And some of the books that were written about him had to hurt a bunch too. I believe what hurt him the most was the hurtful things some family members and close friends said about him; when they thought he was gone and wouldn't know about it. He had done so much for all of them; he loved them. But, they jumped on the band wagon and disgraced him for profit. I truly believe that he sacrificed a lot to keep his family safe, and to serve our country in a noble, but dangerous way.

As a way to respond, to this betrayal, Elvis wrote a letter to, I believe, one of his fan club presidents. You can find it on the internet. I don't believe the date is mentioned and I don't know the name of the fan club or the fan club president, but the letter reads, 'Before I left my thoughts were of all of you. I wanted to leave behind beautiful memories for all of you to share. You see, I knew you loved me, and you would grieve deeply for me. I wanted you to remember me with smiles and love…of a favorite song, concert or dreams.' He went on to say he had always wanted the best for his family, friends, and fans.

He continued, 'Now when I should be at peace, and you should be going onward and growing, I feel so much hate, envy, and jealousy. Instead of leaving beautiful thoughts behind, I find only rubbish going down as guidelines from friends wanting the public to know the truth of the legend known as Elvis Presley. Just what is truth my friends? Is truth calculated as money? Is truth known in friendship? Is truth known in love? Is truth known in caring? Just what is it? I need to know. I want you to know I gave all of these in loving moments in time. I shared myself, and found out that I shared it with Judas; friends that would turn against me after death who did not have the courage to face me in life. This is a reason for dying? If this is the truth, what must your lies be? I send love and healing to all the people that love me. Thank you for believing in me.'

My eyes leaked when I read his last comments. His words crushed my heart a bit. I have never known the experience of true betrayal, but he certainly did. It was definitely a moisture moment for me. I imagine you can feel his pain and sadness, just as I did. My heart sings knowing he has the faith he needs believing he will get through and past it all.

I allowed him to make me a 'mental mess,' and to this day I haven't the slightest idea why it happened, but I still believe it had something to do with the 'shock factor.'

Elvis has such a good heart, and has shown his kindness numerous times. I wish when I had the chance, I would have said to him, 'Thank you for sharing your talent and thank you for touching my life.'

I have often wondered if he had plastic surgery to change his looks. I hope he didn't feel it was necessary to do, but if he did he would still have his unique voice. It would seem a bit 'sacrilegious' to change that…and a bit dangerous too. And regardless of what he looks like he will always be the Elvis we all know; the one who shared his talent at a tremendous cost to him; the one who deserved so much more from all of us than he got. I imagine it would have helped him if the masses would have given him some breathing room. God Bless you, Elvis.

It still amazes me that he has popped into my mind so often through the years. I have relived it many times, and sometimes I wonder if it was a curse instead of a blessing. I wonder if he's still on the planet. He sure could be; because I am. And if he is, he has done a great job of staying somewhat hidden. I imagine there have been sightings and possibly encounters, such as mine, that I haven't heard about. If so, I hope those people handled it a lot better than I did, but more importantly, I hope they haven't found it as difficult to live with as I have.

There have been times that I heard Lisa Marie, Priscilla, or someone else swear that Elvis died August 16, 1977. I just smile and say, "Sure." And other times they manufacture such a story that I want to 'smack em.' I do understand though, and I imagine it has become more difficult for them to answer questions, because Elvis seems determined to let us know he is still in this wonderful world with us. Well, I'm not so sure how wonderful it is today, but it's all we have.

In the early years, I imagine Priscilla had to go along with the lie to support the decision that was made in regard to that day in August. However, after all these years, it seems to me the threat of harm to any of them, by persons unknown to us, would no longer be a threat. I imagine it has been difficult to keep it a secret for so long, but after a while perhaps it was second nature.

I was excited to hear the US Postal Service was issuing an Elvis stamp in January, 1993. I thought they would someday be embarrassed that they had issued a stamp for someone before they died, and then the stamp would have more value. They, of course, didn't have a clue that he was alive. It sure must have come up in conversation when they began to consider it. I wonder if they contacted Lisa Marie to tell her what their plans were. She was almost twenty-five years of age and would surely have discussed it with Priscilla. Perhaps they simply didn't know how to keep the stamp from being issued. They certainly weren't going to say, 'He's not dead yet.' They probably never thought of the penalty for allowing it to happen. By that time they might have figured they would never be found out by the masses. I haven't a clue what kind of penalty would be assessed, but it would be interesting. I don't see that anyone was hurt by issuing it, even though it should not have been done. This reminds me of the saying, 'There is a first time for everything.' In any case, the stupid part of me bought sixty-five sheets, plus several first day issues. I sent family and friends a first day issue stamp. I wonder if any were saved. I still have mine. I spent way more than I should have because I spent every last dollar I had. However, if I could have, I would have purchased more.

The stamp is large, so there is only forty in a sheet. Since Elvis hasn't made an entrance, I suppose my stamps are only worth what I paid for them. The cost to send a first class letter was thirty-nine cents at that time.

One summer afternoon, sometime in 1996 to 1998, I was setting in the Dimond Mall; beside a kiosk a friend of mine owned. He was in the beanie baby secondary market. I had made arrangements to meet him at a certain time. I noticed a group of five men entering the mall. They stood out like a sore thumb. I immediately had a gut feeling. They were dressed in dark suits. It is unusual for men to wear suits in Anchorage except when going to church, funerals, and weddings. And even then many men don't wear them.

I watched them walk on into the mall, and when they got within a few steps from me, they came to a screeching halt. I heard one of them say something, but didn't hear what was said. The minute they stopped they swarmed around one of them... as if to protect. The one, who was directly in front of me, had his back to me. He quickly turned and looked directly at me; our eyes locked. He looked at me with a questioning look. I'm not sure why, but I felt a bit uncomfortable and nervous. He turned completely around and continued to stare at me. I said, "Hi! What are you doing?"

He replied, "We're going to do some auditions." I told him that sounded interesting. In the meantime, the others walked on slowly. I asked him where they were going to do them, and he said, "I'm not sure, but someplace in the Mall."

I smiled and said, "I wish I could listen to them, but I don't have time."

He smiled and turned, saying, "I'd better catch up."

I didn't see his face, but I was sure Elvis/Jon was the person they hovered around. I thought about following them, but I was hurt. It was obvious he didn't want me to see him. I imagine he was as amazed as I was. The odds of that happening again were, once again, one in zillions. I was surprised that he recognized me. And I was surprised that he reacted the way he did because I'm sure he placed the ad in the personals. Perhaps he changed his mind in that length of time.

What surprised me the most was that he was out among us during daylight hours. He must have felt pretty secure that he wouldn't be recognized. Sometimes I wish I would have found the auditions after I met with my friend. I did have time. I just said that I didn't, so he would tell Elvis he didn't have to worry.

If they hadn't stopped so quickly, and the one guy hadn't turned to look at me…it wouldn't have played out the way that it did. I wasn't concentrating on faces, and with them walking together they could easily pass by, and turn into the mall. It did show me Elvis/Jon was still being cautious of what was happening around him. Gads! It's a shame he has to always be looking over his shoulder; so to speak. The fact they were in suits, doing auditions, and uncomfortable with seeing me, did add up to more than speculation that it was Elvis.

I so wish I was more assertive, but once again I didn't want to put him in an uncomfortable situation, and I was hurt because he must have felt he couldn't trust me.

I was amazed and excited that he was in Anchorage. I asked myself, 'Has he been here all these years?' Anchorage could be one of the places he lived, but I was surprised that we were in the same place at the same time once again. I imagine he was too.

May 22, 2007, I returned to the 'lower forty-eight.' It was a bit difficult to leave the beautiful state of Alaska after twenty-one years, but Alabama is also a beautiful state.

Four

Elvis/Jesse

Sometime in 2003, my daughter, Jami Lynn, asked me to write my bio. She suggested it would be a nice gift for my grandchildren. It sounded like a bigger project than I could accomplish. However, with her encouragement, a year later I bought a computer and began writing, '*What I Remember Before I Forget*.' It amazes me that I have remembered so much. It is quite lengthy because I have covered seventy-six years.

After I got settled in my new shelter I continued writing. When I got to chapter thirty-five I had mixed emotions about including this memory. I didn't want to create a problem for Elvis/Jon, but I didn't think it was right to leave it out because of the title. I prayed about it lots before my decision was made to include it, but I still hesitated. Even though he told me I could share my experience I felt like I would be betraying him. I wished that I knew if he was still living.

My granddaughter, Brittany, informed me I could do a Google search on just about anything simply by typing a word or two into the search space. After having my computer four years I had not used the internet other than for emails and my writing. When I typed in, 'Elvis Presley,' I was astonished at all the information that appeared. I sat here shaking my head and thinking, 'who knew?'

I hoped to locate the book Elvis said he had started. Larry Geller's book, 'If I Can Dream,' caught my attention because it said, 'Elvis' own story.' I thought it just might be the book Elvis meant, so I ordered it. I could hardly wait for it to arrive. In the meantime I continued to find interesting articles about him.

In my search somehow I found EIN (Elvis Information Network.) I couldn't believe my eyes. I discovered a page where Elvis fans talked to each other. In fact, more than that, I soon learned they actually argued with each other. Some of them used very bad language and many were hateful to each other. And the arguments were about....Is Elvis alive? I continued to read, but did not voice my opinion because I didn't want to involve myself in such ridiculous and ignorant conversation. I think it is so very sad that anyone treats another person as they do. And I am confident that Elvis would not want to be the subject of this kind of conversation. Even though I didn't like what was happening on EIN I continued to sign in to see what was being said....hoping the conversation would change to something that was fun to read, but it continued to be hateful, mean-spirited, and depressing.

During my search, I learned about a book titled 'The Truth About Elvis Aron Presley, In His Own Words.' The author is Donald Hinton, M. D. with "Jesse," and was printed by American Literary Press, Inc.

I thought since Elvis hadn't made an official appearance he may have made arrangements to have it published after he went on to bigger and better things. What I didn't understand is why I hadn't heard about it when it was published in 2001. Surely, this was a perfect way for Elvis to let the general public know he had not died in 1977, and it would explain all that his fans want to know. And yet here it is 2010, and I am just now hearing about it. Something just wasn't right.

It wasn't easy to find this book. However, I did; and I patiently waited to get it. I knew it would be a book that I wouldn't put down until I finished reading it. I was sure it would hold my interest as did the book, 'Is Elvis Alive?'

The book arrived after a few days; I was immediately disgruntled. I expected a nice size book, but it is only eighty-eight pages, and measures one-fourth inch thick. I was totally disappointed. Before I even turned a page, I knew it was going to leave a lot to be desired. How on earth could the truth about Elvis be published in a mere one-fourth inch? And why on earth would this book look so tacky? Did I expect too much? I don't think so. I think any fan would expect a first class bound book if it was in Elvis's own words. It was clear this would be a quick read. I hoped it would be more interesting than it looked. So I began reading.

It's very interesting....very interesting, indeed. However, after reading it I believe you would be as disappointed as I am.

Before I go any further I want you to know that this book is written by Dr. Hinton with Elvis, as Jesse, giving him the information for it. It was a gift; actually, a priceless gift. Elvis wanted the truth told, and he trusted Dr. Hinton to write and publish it. He knew the doctor would make a great deal of money from the sales of the book, and that is what he wanted. It was his way of showing appreciation for the kindness the doctor had shown him. Elvis wanted him to keep the cost as low as possible so it would be affordable to anyone. The price of the book was twelve dollars ninety-five cents in the United States and five dollars more in Canada. I located the book at a much higher price.

Thinking back, I realize I worked two jobs at that time, and in June of that year I went to work at a gold mine. It was a remote site position, and I was out of Anchorage four to seven weeks at a time, and home or traveling for two or three weeks. I seldom heard anything about Elvis, unless there was something on TV, or a story about him in one of the tabloids. I wish someone would have told me about it since I knew, without any doubt, that Elvis did not die in 1977.

Dr. Hinton included several letters that Elvis wrote to him. And in almost every letter he tells the doctor that he can ask him any questions he wants to. He makes it clear that he wants the truth of his life told after he has actually died. I don't know how they met or when, but Elvis apparently trusted him to finish the project and follow his instructions.

Elvis says in the introduction that he decided to tell the world the real story after hearing so many stories about his death. He also says, "Many people have written about my death as a hoax. It was not a hoax." He explains that he decided to reinvent himself in the form of his twin, Jesse Garon, who died at birth. And therefore, he says, "Elvis Presley did die that day." And of course he is speaking of August 16, 1977.

At first this was difficult to wrap my brain around, but by the time I finished the book I understood where he was coming from. He had a close spiritual connection to Jesse, and it troubled him to know that Jesse didn't have the opportunity to live his life, while Elvis reaped the rewards of being one of the most magnificent talents of our time; if not the most talented.

Elvis always thought Jesse deserved to live. I'm not a twin, so I don't know how I would have felt if I were in the same situation. However, I do believe there was a reason why Jesse didn't have the chance for life on earth while Elvis was here. It's just possible that Jesse was chosen for bigger and better things. In any case, sometime through the years Elvis took the name of, Jesse, and let him live his life as the brother of a celebrity. It sounds a bit weird, but I guess we would have to walk in Elvis's shoes to fully understand why he says he is now nothing more than a man who had a very famous brother.

It's easy for us, the common man, to think it would be great to live the life of Elvis Presley. He had everything he wanted, and he had the money to buy anything he could possibly dream of; anyway, anything that was for sale. However, it all came at a tremendous price that was beyond money.

It seems strange that he would become depressed and lonely, living in such a lifestyle, but he did. And just like so many of us, this caused him to put on extra pounds that created health issues that required prescription drugs; some of which could have also caused him to gain even more weight. He didn't like his appearance anymore than we do when we are overweight. However, he didn't hide away like many of us do. He was an entertainer, and he wanted to continue giving as much to us as he could. We couldn't possibly know how much he was hurting, but I am betting, at times, he thought it was more than he could bear.

I learned that Elvis studies numerology, and that he closely follows his chart. He says, "Anyone who studies numerology will understand; those who don't may want to look into it." I know nothing about it, and hope to look into it when I have the time. I imagine it is one of those things I will have to pencil in, and make time for, or I would never get it done. In any case, he says August 16, 1977 was the perfect day.

He asks his fans to forgive him. He says it sounds corny, but it was the only way to give Jesse life.

He says the colonel was a loyal friend, and took this secret to his grave. I'm glad, because at times I thought the colonel demanded too much of Elvis, and that he made some decisions that weren't in Elvis's best interest. It goes to show us that we can speculate and speculate some more, but we still don't know what is in someone else's heart and mind. Elvis signed the introduction, Sincerely, Jesse Presley.

I am befuddled when he says, "But I will no longer stand by and have people like Gail Brewer tell you stories that are pure fiction." He says his death was not a hoax. The definition of a hoax is to deceive, to trick into believing, or accepting as genuine something false and often preposterous. Some synonyms of the word are; deception, fraud, and fake. I use the word, 'faked,' several times in my story about him. It seems to me, it is the same as using the word hoax. I'm surprised that Elvis would say this about Gail because in everything I have read of hers, she has not once put him down. However, she is the person who started the majority of people asking the question, "Is Elvis Alive?" but we all should be grateful to her for spending so much time doing the research that was required to accomplish such a project.

According to Gail, there were no books written about Elvis before hers, so with her books and some reported sightings of Elvis, it started a whirlwind investigation. And it has continued through the years. So that had to give Elvis much stress. For this I am sorry…truly sorry…that we caused him to say, on August 2, 1998, "…and I thought I could have a normal life."

Dr. Hinton includes copies of the letters he received from Elvis. It is clearly his handwriting. However, a handwriting analysis was done to prove it is Elvis's writing.

Elvis is sixty-three years of age when he writes in a letter dated April 20, 1998, that he would be honored for the doctor to write his memoirs so that, after his passing, his fans would know why he did what he did. He says he wants his fans to know that he probably would not have lived if he continued the way he had been living.

He says the colonel had the plan. And some people who were close to him were sure they could pull it off. He was going into debt bad and his health was deteriorating. It's true; the plan made Elvis's estate very wealthy. However, Elvis could not have known that would happen, nor did he know so many people truly loved him and his talent. It is amazing that the numbers grow each year at Graceland.

It seems a bit humorous to me that he isn't allowed any cash; because 'they' think with his proliferative ways he could make people curious. He is given nearly everything he needs, but he has no access to cash. He says that everything used to go to him at an address that he does not share, but people were stealing from him and reading his mail…even taking his medication. No wonder he has a difficult time trusting anyone.

He tells the doctor that he will continue to tell him about his life since 1977, so he can document it; he will provide information that only Elvis would know; and why he is now Jesse. He signs the letter, Sincerely, Jesse 'Elvis.'

In the 'Forward' Dr. Hinton says Elvis has not yet passed away, and that he is sixty-six years of age. At that time, he says it has been twenty-four years since Elvis's life ended and Jesse's began. If that is the case, it was 1977 when he began using the name of Jesse. Perhaps Doctor Hinton thought he began using it then, but he didn't tell me his name was, Jesse.

Dr. Hinton says he has been living in two different realties for several years. In one, which he shares with most people, Elvis is dead, despite the many rumors. In the other, he lived with the secret that Elvis is alive. I can identify with the stress this put on him, but he was faithful to Elvis. He treated Elvis's chronic pain for four years.

It was June 30, 1997, when the doctor learned Elvis was alive. He received a phone call from a friend who felt in her heart that the doctor could be trusted with this truth. They had known each other ten years, and had developed a friendship. This is when he learned Elvis was living as Jesse. This friend is referred to as 'Shuma,' and she told him she began communicating with Elvis in 1991. Before then she was doing a newsletter about Elvis. The doctor was just beginning his medical practice after finishing his residency a year earlier.

Elvis's chronic pain started in the early 1970's. August, 1977, NBC did a special report on the discovery of his medical problems. It was said that he suffered compression fractures in his spine, and he still performed one hundred thirty-six shows for his fans over a period of ten months in 1974. I believe it is absolutely incredible that he put himself through such a grueling schedule.

Dr. Hinton said Elvis is a kind and gentle soul.... always giving. Getting to know him has been the most wonderful experience of his life. Elvis showed his gratitude with many cards, letters, and gifts. It made him happy to know that Elvis was well, and receiving good and appropriate medical care given the circumstances.

I can imagine helping Elvis gave him a really great feeling. He had idolized Elvis since he was a very young boy. I believe he said he was eleven years of age when his father told him Elvis had died, and they cried together. And now here he was with an unbelievable opportunity to be of service to him.

September 8, 1997, Elvis wrote a letter to Dr. Hinton and simply signed it, Thank you, 'E.' At this time, there was a person or company, name not mentioned, that offered a ten million dollar reward to anyone who could produce substantial evidence that Elvis is still alive. Can you imagine how difficult it must have been for Elvis? It seems to me hundreds of people would be looking for him to collect the reward. Privacy must have always been a premium for him.

In November 1997, Elvis sent a picture of himself with his Grandson, Benjamin Storm, setting on his lap on a riding lawnmower. Benjamin was born October 21, 1992. He appears to be around three years old. So, Elvis was around sixty years of age in this picture.

It is said that Elvis has had lots of plastic surgeries to change his appearance. The doctor says the combination of normal aging and the plastic surgery has dramatically changed his appearance. Dr. Hinton says he was sad for Elvis because of all that he had to endure just to try to find peace. I imagine many others feel as Dr. Hinton does. I know I do.

I believe when you first see the picture you will not see a resemblance to Elvis at all. So absolutely no one would know it was Elvis....unless they heard him speak. I still have a difficult time wrapping my brain around this knowledge. It doesn't seem logical that Elvis would change his appearance, and then want to share it with us before his death. This is why I am sure he did not want the book published until after his death. It wouldn't surprise me if he had more surgery after Dr. Hinton published the book, so that now he wouldn't look like he does in the picture. But, what would I know about what he would or wouldn't do?

As the months passed during that first year, Dr. Hinton said trust and communication increased at a tremendous rate. Elvis wanted to begin work on his story. He wrote another letter dated September 18, 1998. He said, "I want you sir, to write me with any questions you might have, so we can get to writing this book." He goes on to say, "One fact that most people would think is that my Daddy must have known....well he didn't. We were planning on telling him when he passed away without ever knowing."

I was sure his Daddy knew. I bet Vernon got quite a surprise to learn Elvis was not with Gladys to greet him. I doubt they would have panicked. However, for at least a split second, I imagine they held their breath.

Elvis said they intentionally left many clues in 1977, so that some people could find out. He also says he has lived in many places, and that one person has come close to finding him. This person has pictures, but they have no real evidence, as far as he knows. In my search, I learned who the person was in one of the books I read. You will learn about this later.

Elvis says again that he has so many restrictions on him. When he asks for cash he is given the third degree on what he needs the cash for. He signs this letter, Sincerely, Jesse.

In November 1998 Elvis told the doctor that he started thinking about faking his death in 1974. Yeah! He uses the same term as I do, so I don't feel bad now.

I imagine you have heard that it is believed by many that it was a wax figure in Elvis's coffin. For those people who don't know Elvis is alive, I'm sure it is hard to believe such a thing. None-the-less, there is much evidence that it was. For instance, more than one person at the viewing said the body in the casket was perspiring. The temperature in Memphis was quite hot, but it is impossible for a dead body to perspire.

Finally, now we know. Elvis says when he first saw a wax figure of him made by a Mr. Cooper, he was fascinated with it. He asked Mr. Cooper if he could make another one for him. Mr. Cooper said he could. Elvis placed the order, and told him to keep it strictly confidential. I must say, Mr. Cooper did a lousy job on the nose. It clearly didn't look like Elvis. Elvis said he mentioned it to a few close friends. A few are more than two, but he only names Joe Esposito and Larry Geller. In any case, they didn't think he was serious.

Elvis says he was tired of being Elvis Presley. Once again, he said his health was deteriorating, and he couldn't keep up. His finances were floundering because of his Daddy's poor business ventures. He was simply at his wit's end.

He said that as the years progressed he had ups and downs, and says they are pretty well documented in other books. He originally picked 1976, to fake his death, but he chickened out. He said a pact was made on the grounds of Graceland one night, with those being present placing hands over hands, and promising this secret would never be spoken of outside the room they were in. Originally only four were involved, one being Elvis, and they kept the secret.

He knew that when his book arrived in bookstores his loyal friends would be heartbroken, because they had taken care of him, and convinced others that he was no longer alive. He repeats that, in reality, Elvis Presley died that day and his twin brother, Jesse, came to life; living in hiding, but as a normal person.

He says Lisa Marie was told months later, and was told she wouldn't see her Daddy very much. At one point he says his thoughts are scrambled, and again tells the doctor to ask him all the questions he wants about anything, and then to put it in order so it makes sense. In the spring of 1998, Elvis spent some time in Florida to be near Lisa Marie. She owned a home in Clearwater, Florida.

He says, "Many people believe me to still be alive, but I was told in the beginning, there would be no contact in order for this to work." He also says, "My personal thoughts are that my fans will understand. That is very important to me."

I was surprised when I read, "I just could not face myself any more after seeing myself in the mirror, and that is where Larry Geller came in. He asked if he could write a book, and I gave him my blessing. *'If I Can Dream,'* is the title, and I liked his book."

Elvis says Larry filled his head with spiritual thoughts, and made him believe they could pull off faking his death. Elvis thought if he had stayed any longer he would have been booed off the stage. I could never imagine this ever happening, because like I said earlier, he has such magnetism that just the sight of him at a concert was worth the price of a ticket.

He said he was very nervous on August 16, 1977, but it had to be done before he went on the road, because he wouldn't have been able to pull it off. Then he asks, "Did you know there are secret compartments in Graceland that very few people know about?"

He said he was given an injection that looked like he was dead, but the people closest to him knew better. And it worked, so he became, Jesse, a poor white southern boy who didn't sing a lick of anything. This letter is signed, Your Pal, Jesse.

He could have given us many more details about this time and perhaps he would have. However, the book was published before he intended it to be.

In the letter he wrote January 25, 1999, he says he was told publishers' fees are enormous. I have been told the same thing, and that the publisher is the one who receives most of the price of a book, and there is not much left for the author.

He talks about being involved in police work. He participated in a bust in Denver and one in

Miami. However, he was recognized in Miami, so all the police work he thought he would do was brought to a halt. The people he worked with determined it would not be safe for him to continue, even after his extensive plastic surgery.

He says he has lived in a dozen cities since 1977, and not all were warm. He adds, Boise, Idaho was the worst and Hawaii was the best.

He said, "It is my voice that gives everything away, and people have said to me, you sound like Elvis." Well, duh! This is why it seems to me bazaar that he would do extensive surgery when he would never be able to change his voice. I suppose he could simply not speak, but that would be extremely difficult.

At the age of sixty-four he watches a lot of videos and is into several collections. He signs this letter; Sincerely, Jesse.

He wouldn't write Dr. Hinton again until May 13, 1999. He says he is listing seven of the locations he has lived since, 1977. They are: Alvin, TX, Geneva, IL, Apopka, FL, Litchfield Park, AZ, Pittsburgh, PA, Tenino, WA, and Warren, OH. He makes a comment that Apopka is nice, and he stayed only two weeks in Pittsburg. He says there are several more, but he couldn't think of them at that moment. I can't believe he would ever forget Anchorage or anywhere else he lived in Alaska; one of which I believe is Kodiak Island.

In this letter, he said the Graceland estate does not let him contact them personally. They are determined to keep the myth alive, and don't want him taking any chances. He said he had recently asked for a donation to help the Oklahoma people who had lost everything in the tornado that struck ten days earlier. They were reluctant, but finally said they would make a donation through the estate. A very destructive tornado hit Oklahoma on May 3, 1999.

During a phone conversation with Elvis on July 24, 1999, he stated he had something he wanted put in the book, and added that it was the most important thing he wanted his fans to know, after all this time. He restated that what happened on August 16, 1977, was not a hoax. Elvis Presley died on that day, and he has been living his life as, Jesse, whose spiritual presence has been inside of him ever since he was a young boy.

He talks about his writing being terrible; it is, but lots of people don't take the time to put their words on paper neatly. All he has to do is practice, practice, practice, and his writing would look completely different. However, he didn't put 'practice writing' on his 'priority' list, and there is nothing wrong with that. He can at least feel good that he wrote legibly. It certainly isn't difficult to read his writing.

I was sure Elvis went into the Witness Protection Program in 1977, and then he couldn't handle the seclusion, so he chose to try to stay 'unnoticed.' And I believe he has done a great job overall. However, he says he chose not to go into the program, because, if he had, he would have absolutely no communication with anyone. And he wanted to give Jesse a chance to live.

At this point, as I read, it continued to seem a little strange to me, and so I was still having a bit of a problem wrapping my brain around it.

He once again tells Dr. Hinton that he trusts 'them' to write the book, and that he wants 'them' to ask anything they want to for the book. He repeats the purpose for the book is to tell his fans that this was not a hoax, but necessary. He says the last two years of his life as Elvis, 1976 and 1977, were miserable. He had quit communicating with most of his true friends, and he mentioned, Johnny Cash. He was in deep depression.

This tells me I was right on the mark. Elvis handled his appearance no different than most of us do. He withdrew from his friends; they didn't withdraw from him. I'm sure he wanted to withdraw from the whole world. He was a mental mess, and dealt with it the best that he could, and for as long as he could. Like I said, I can identify with his behavior, and there is no doubt in my mind that many of you can too.

Elvis told Dr. Hinton he was surprised that so many people suspected, from the beginning, that he was still alive, but with a few trusted friends they had been able to get away with it for so long.

He talks more about numerology, and now I really want to learn about it. It amazes me because he says he has followed his chart explicitly, and that he can predict his future with it. I'm not sure I want to know what my future has in store for me. However, without knowing anything about numerology, I predict my future will be exactly as it is supposed to be. I am confident that when it is my turn to return to our Heavenly Father it will be the best journey I have ever had. What could be better than that?

Elvis mentions he is not happy with the results of his plastic surgery. He writes about this almost eleven years ago, and it totally blows my mind that he would actually even think about changing his voice. However, he says, "We are working on a way I can alter my voice to get rid of my thick southern accent."

He says that even though many people still believe he is alive he became more daring, and began going out with minimal disguises. He adds that he just didn't talk much.

He tells the doctor that his relationship with him, Shuma and her husband has created much jealousy with his buddies. His buddies say they have known Elvis longer, so they think they should get 'top billing.' He says, "I hope your book is a huge success," and signs the letter, with warm regards, Jesse.

A few weeks later he sent Dr. Hinton a Christmas gift. He and another person had to retrieve them from his Graceland bedroom late one night, because 'they' did not want him within five miles of Graceland. Dr. Hinton says many times he had thought, 'if the world only knew.'

In his first letter of 2000, he expresses that he wants to get the book finished. He is well aware that he is sixty-five, and concerned that he is, 'getting up there in years.' He says his right hand shakes uncontrollably sometimes. He doesn't know why because he hasn't seen a doctor about it. He wants to know if the Dr. would prefer that he print his letters. Dr. Hinton has shown us the letters and Elvis's writing is still legible.

He still feels bad that he didn't have the opportunity to tell his Daddy. The plan was to wait three years, but his Daddy died six months before that time.

He finally reveals that it was Herb Wolff and his wife, and Howard Hughes, who had the means to pull off his disappearance. Herb is a Las Vegas Billionaire. Add that to the brilliant mind of the Colonel, and it was a done deal.

I would like to bring it to your attention that it was reported Howard Hughes died April 05, 1976. It has since been learned he too didn't like living in the public eye. He hired a mentally incompetent man to impersonate him while he conducted his business in peace from Panama with a new wife. It was unfortunate that the stand in lived life as an unkempt recluse because that is the wrap Howard got, but in the bigger picture it made little difference to Howard because he was living his life the way he wanted to. He actually died, November 21, 2001, in Alabama. This is another interesting story. You might want to check it out. I recommend the book, 'Boxes,' written by Douglas Wellman. It was published by WriteLife, LLC., in 2001. As with Elvis, there were several stories through the years that Howard did not die in 1976.

Elvis wanted to give the doctor something that has never been published. Perhaps so the readers will believe his story. He asks, "Did you know that every person that passed in front of my casket had one thing in common? They all made the same statement when asked about my state when they looked at me in my coffin. Even my relatives said it. They said, "It doesn't look like him." Apparently someone had been instructed to place a concealed recorder near the casket. He signs the letter, Sincerely, Jesse.

In March 2000, he shared something he thought was important for the book. He thought it was definite evidence that he didn't die in 1977. The night of August 15, 1977, he went to his dentist and had his gold tooth removed. He said that anyone close to him would remember that he had one. He thought it should be done since he was no longer going to be Elvis. He kept it, but now wanted to give it to Dr. Hinton. I have read elsewhere that Elvis had two gold teeth.

At this time, he told Dr. Hinton that he couldn't trust everyone around him. He had become aware of a conspiracy to steal the tooth and sell it to a jeweler, 'for a whole lot of money.' He decided before that could happen he would send it to the doctor to be included in his book. The doctor received it shortly before Easter. As with all the items that Elvis sent to him, there is a picture in the book, and he reports the history of the gift.

Dr. Hinton remarried the summer of 2000. At this time Elvis made a trip to Chicago to attend a gospel music review. He sent Dr. Hinton several gifts for his upcoming wedding and for his recent birthday. One of the gifts was the walking cane Elvis had used for quite some time. Now this is the one item I would have liked. I'm sure it wasn't nearly as expensive as all the other gifts, and also not as valuable as a collectible, but I think it would be absolutely marvelous to have a useable gift that Elvis used; one that he often touched.

September 20, 2000, Elvis wrote another letter to Dr. Hinton. This is interesting, because he heads it with, four a.m. Austin time.' He had recently finished reviewing the book in its incomplete form. He begins with, "Great book!" It's good to know he approved of the contents up to that time, and he must have liked how it was done. He continues, "You did a great job. The changes I want to make are as such." However, Dr. Hinton doesn't share what the changes are.

Elvis says, "Remember you will come under a lot of scrutiny by stating my life. Also, most importantly, do you want to use your name and address?"Elvis tells him he will be hounded, and he doesn't want him to be plagued with problems. Elvis says he has already been told that Lisa Marie will cause problems if B. J.'s picture is shown. He is concerned about the doctor because he has a good job and a great family, and he doesn't want the doctor to jeopardize it.

He continues to say that many of his people and so called friends have learned about the book and are jealous and unhappy. They expected to make money off of the truth of Elvis's life. I am laughing here, because I can see in my mind the hustle and bustle of all these people trying to get their book published first; after Elvis actually returns to our Heavenly Father.

You would think they would be the ones going through a mourning period before they would even think about a book. In any case, it is Elvis's life, and he can still make 'some' of his own decisions. Since he chose the doctor to get his book written and published, they should simply accept it. We humans are so strange.

He says he has many more intimate secrets to tell and invites them to ask about whatever they want to know. He comments that Shuma and Bern are as equally important to him, and calls them 'his trinumerate.' I believe this is the first time I have heard the word, 'trinumerate.'

He says he is still in good health, and contributes it to the fact that they give him undying loyalty, and he says it is especially helpful to him. He signs this letter, Sincerely, Jesse G. Presley.

Dr. Hinton received another letter on October 20, 2000. In this letter, he tells us that he picked the most naïve person he could think of to discover his body. It was Ginger Alden, but he adds that she waited way too long. I did not understand what he meant when he said she waited too long. However, now I do. In another book it was said the body had begun to go into rigor mortise. So we know, at this point, there was a body.... not a wax figure; but whose? It really doesn't matter as long as a crime wasn't committed. He says he believes anyone who knew of his predicaments at the time, and had any sympathy for his lifestyle, will forgive him for what he did.

He tells the doctor he worries that writing the book will hurt the doctor's reputation, and says he wouldn't be angry if he didn't want to continue with it.

He goes on to say he has instructions in a safe deposit box that tell his four friends, Dr. Hinton, Shuma, Sloan, and Bern to cremate his body and spread his ashes around the home in Tupelo. He continues to say he is still healthy. He signs this letter, Your Pal, Jesse

The result must have been that Elvis decided not to wait until his death for the book to come out. Since numerology is very important to him... the year 2001 is significant. I also imagine his curiosity got the best of him; he wanted to see for himself what the results would be. I say this because Dr. Hinton says he made initial contact with the publisher in December, 2000, with Elvis's permission.

Not once did Dr. Hinton tell us if he asked Elvis questions, or what they were if he did. Elvis had so much to tell us, and I am really disappointed that the information was not shared; since he said that Dr. Hinton could ask him anything. It seems to me the other people in the group could also have told Dr. Hinton to ask some of their questions. The book would have been more interesting, and certainly could use the additional content.

If Elvis would have told me I could ask him anything I wanted to, I would have asked him: Would you confirm when you left Graceland and Memphis and where did you go, how long did you stay, and at that time did you have anyone living with you, and who were they?

Were you the person behind the screen at Graceland? Were you shocked when you saw the picture? The person who took the picture later said that he did not think it was you. Did the Presley Estate have anything to do with him changing his mind?

Did you ask Priscilla to go with you, so that you could still be active in Lisa Marie's life? What did Priscilla tell you when you told her of your plans? How long did you wait before you contacted her? Would you tell us about your meetings with Lisa Marie? What ages was she and where did you meet? Was it difficult explaining to her why you were doing what you were doing? Did she ever tell you she felt bad about lying? Did you attend her weddings? If so, did you disguise yourself as a relative? Did you feel bad that you couldn't walk her down the · aisle? How old were your grandchildren when you first saw them? How did you feel when you learned you were going to be a grandpa, or like they say in the south, paw paw?

When did your first sighting occur and where were you? Did you feel threatened? Did you move around a lot because you were recognized or was this your original plan?

You mentioned living in one place for only two weeks. That sounds like a vacation to me. Did something happen there that made you decide to move on? Would you tell us all the places you have lived, and the length of time you stayed?

When did you meet someone whom you were interested enough in to develop a relationship?

How many relationships have you had since 1977? How long did each of them last? Do you have any contact with any of them now? How did you meet them? Did you meet their family, and did they treat you as a regular guy after they got over the shock? Was it difficult for you to think they wouldn't tell others about you? Did you have any children with anyone other than Priscilla? If so are they included in your will?

Did you swear people, who became close to you, to secrecy? After you dissolved your relationship how did you handle it when you learned they had told your story?

I recall seeing a picture in a tabloid of a young lady setting by a tree with a child. She said she had lived with you for about two or three years. Is this true?

I know Christmas is a special time for you. What year were you speaking about when you said you were going to shock some people at Christmas by making an appearance?

Were you visiting your girlfriend's family, or your family, and in what city was it in? Did your girlfriend ease the shock somehow before you arrived? Would you tell us about those experiences? Was any of your family angry that they had not been told of your plan in 1977?

I imagine you read or were told about tabloid stories about you. Are there any that particularly concerned you? And would you tell us why?

Did you put a personal ad in the Anchorage newspaper asking me to call you? Did you see me setting in the Dimond mall eight or ten years after our Safeway moments? Why didn't you take a deep breath and walk over to me with a friendly smile? You knew I didn't tell any media about you the first time we met, so why did you think I might this time?

What hobbies or collections are you interested in?

How many people do you have on your payroll? Are any of them from your old group in Memphis? Did you interview for their positions? Were they shocked to see who they would be working for?

How have you handled your banking all these years? Does the Presley Estate pay your employees? Do you pay top wages hoping to win their silence? Have you had each of them sign a statement saying they will keep silent about you until you have truly gone on to bigger and better things?

Have you been confined in a hospital since 1977, and if so, where were you at the time? What name did you use? Did anyone become suspicious or tell you that you look like Elvis Presley? If so, how did you get through those times?

What did you do to keep yourself busy? Was it fun to retire at forty-two, and do what you wanted to do? Did you ever get bored? Has it been easy being the boss, or have you let friendship interfere with your working relationship?

Have you had enough plastic surgery that you no longer have to look over your shoulder? For instance, can you finally go out in public and feel totally relaxed, and simply be Jesse Presley?

Did you ever live on Kodiak Island? If so, how long, and when were you there? Where did you live in other parts of Alaska? Was it one of your major homes? Did you find the temperature in Anchorage much gentler than some places in the 'lower-forty-eight?'

Who was the young lady at the Safeway store who asked you if you got the jalapeno peppers? Were you afraid to return with your entourage? Who gave the order to pull the book, 'Orion,' from bookstores? Was the same thing tried with the book, 'Is Elvis Alive?' What did you think of it? Were you surprised that Gail had such great information for us, and that she shared her research? Were you angry because she published her findings? Do you now realize she did a wonderful service to your fans and the world at large? Did you think she was simply out to make money? Why would you fault her for making money? It is expensive to publish, and we all need to earn a living. Is it different than your concerts? Tickets aren't free. Do you know that she has never written anything negative about you? Did you have the book, 'The Presley Arrangement,' written by Monte Wayne Nicholson removed from the bookshelves? Now that you are a senior citizen do you want to live closer to Lisa Marie and your grandchildren? Couldn't that happen, and you still have privacy, simply by not talking to the media?

Will you tell us what music you have done that is available for your fans to purchase? When was it completed? Did you ever get the old gang together like you hoped to? How did you do it? What were the reactions you received? It appears; there are many people who know you did not die in 1977. How have you managed to keep most of them quiet?

It appears your 'trinumerate,' have broken up their friendship of so many years. How do you feel about this? Have you tried to persuade them to forgive each other, and not let the friendship fail? Do you think some of it was caused from jealousy being shown near the release of the book? Do you still keep in contact with the three of them? Since they are no longer close, can you trust them to follow through with your cremation? In the final scheme of things, wouldn't Lisa Marie be the best person to take care of your cremation, or possibly the lady you live with? Since you have already had the humongous funeral, don't you think either of them could and would handle your cremation in private, so that no one would know it was done?

Are you angry at the way the book was released? Did you trust the doctor to know how to advertise it, and it didn't happen? Since there is so much information missing from Dr. Hinton's book have you made arrangements with Lisa Marie or one of your grandchildren to write the book with all the unanswered questions, and the things you wanted included? Since I didn't know the book was written or released, I don't know how much 'buzz' it got. Were you disappointed? At the time, did you think many of your fans would not be aware of it, or do you think I was one of a few who knew nothing about it?

How did you hear the Postal Service was issuing an Elvis Presley stamp? Did you try to stop it? Did you purchase any of the stamps or have someone purchase them for you? Where did you live when the stamps were released?

Did you have a good view in all the places you have lived? Were you ever comfortable enough to introduce yourself to any neighbors? If so, did you use disguises so they wouldn't know who you were?

You said you wanted to let Jesse live through you, but how could that happen when you couldn't be an average citizen as Jesse would have been? What kind of work would you do in Jesse's name? How could Jesse live a normal life when he had to live in such a secluded way? Could Jesse marry and have a family? Could Jesse have pursued his own dreams, or what you think his dreams would have been? Wouldn't the fact that you had to hide, as Elvis, not allow Jesse to live his life as he would have in normal circumstances?

When did you stop using the name Jon Burrows and take Jesse's name? It appears you learned shortly after August 1977, that it was difficult for you not to sing. Did you get the singing out of your system before you took on the name of Jesse? If not, you continued singing when you were living as Jesse. Do you believe Jesse would have been as talented as you, and that he would also pursue a singing career? I can't image two such talented and charismatic people.

Jesse should have had an easy life since his famous brother was paying for all of his needs and most of his wants? He never really knew what it was like to live without the Presley estate. Elvis, however, did live without excess cash. You had plenty of material things, however you have shown you no longer need or necessarily want them. This I'm sure made your life less complicated, but there was no way either of you could live the life you expected when you made the decision you did in, 1977. Am I right about this?

What vehicles do you presently own? Do you own a motorcycle? Do you go biking with your buddies, or did you in the past when perhaps your back could handle it?

Have you traveled in your own plane since 1977, or have you always traveled on commercial airlines? Did you always have your buddies, and/or girlfriend with you when you traveled? How did you handle it when you were recognized or when someone mentioned Elvis to you?

Would you tell us some of your experiences that have actually made you chuckle?

When you left the Safeway store the morning we met what did you tell your friends? Where did you go? Were you laughing at me when you drove through the parking lot? Did you ever drive or did one of your buddies do the driving? Did your buddies have cars of their own?

Do you have a large house with bedrooms for all of your employees?

Were you ever in non-speaking roles in movies after 1977; and if so what movies? Were you the hobo setting in the corner of the boxcar at the end of the movie, 'The Last Train to Memphis?'

Were you a bit frightened when you heard a humongous reward was offered to the first person who found you and proved that you were alive? How could you relax when you didn't trust the people who worked for you? Did you ever fear one or more may be a 'Judas' or were you confident that anyone who would put themselves in that situation would be despised by most of the world.

Do you have a private cook? If so, does he/she live in? Does he/she know who Jesse really is? It appears you have allowed more and more people to know you did not physically die in, 1977. Have you ever wished you had kept more in hiding, or do you feel you had to live as you have for Jesse to have a chance at life? This still seems a bit mind-boggling to me, but I really do know where you are coming from. I truly do understand.

What is your connection to the singer 'Orion,' Orion Pictures, Jon Cotner, and Doug Church?

This is an enormous amount of questions, and I imagine I would have more if I thought about it for awhile, but these simply flowed out of my mind. And that's the way it is. We really want to know everything about Elvis/Jon/Jesse. Not because it's any of our business; because it's not. It's simply because he touched all our lives in such a way that we seem not to get enough. Maybe one day he will have someone answer these questions, and anything else he wants us to know. And when he is really gone, we will finally know that he shared enough.

Elvis sent two hair samples from 1957 or 1958, to the doctor for Christmas. He thought that would clinch the authenticity of the book, because DNA doesn't lie. He tells the doctor to be careful and discreet with the names in the book, and says that Bern doesn't want his name included. He then asks if he can do something about that. Elvis wondered if the book could be sold through the internet. He signs off with, Take care, your friend, Jesse.

Dr. Hinton says, "There are no words to, sufficiently, describe the physical and emotional journey I have experienced these last four years. It has affected every aspect of my life, but I am a very lucky human being. I did it all out of love for Jesse, and if asked to do it again, I would."

He realizes there will be people who think he is a fake, and says he would have taken the information, in his book, to his grave... if Elvis had wanted him to. I personally don't see how anyone who reads his book could think he was a fake. I guess it's easy for me to say, because of my experience. However, it is impossible not to know it is the truth after reading his book, seeing so many pictures of items that belonged to Elvis, and to read copies of the letters he wrote.

However, there must have been many who didn't believe it, because some people still don't believe he is alive. Could they all have missed the book when it was being sold? Could they have missed the amazing news confirming that he didn't die on August 16, 1977, or was it not on the news? If it wasn't on the news; why wasn't it? Something is missing here. I just don't understand how anyone today doesn't know that he was definitely alive after 1977.

I would like to know what happened with this book, and I would like to know how many copies were printed. I am sending a letter to the American Literary Press, who is the publisher of the book, for permission to use what I have conveyed, and to ask them how the distribution of the book was handled.

I have used the name, Elvis, in my writing about Dr. Hinton's book. However, the doctor almost always used, Jesse.

At the back of the book are four letters. One is written by Dr. Hinton's wife, Heather, that says she supports her husband one hundred percent. She also tells us that it hasn't been easy. Her husband has enjoyed helping Elvis and becoming friends with him, however, with the enjoyment there has been a lot of stress and pressure.

Another is written by Bern, who Elvis mentions often in his book. It is a wonderful story; a story about this man who had an unexpected experience when he met Elvis after 1977. Only his meeting turned into a friendship. I truly believe the same would have happened to me if I would have answered the ad in the personals'. The day after Thanksgiving in 1988, Bern was driving to a city that he doesn't name. He passed through a small farm town, and was nearly to the highway, when he noticed an elderly couple standing beside a blue pick-up truck. He pulled in front of the truck to see if he could help them. He noticed a younger man in the middle of the cab. He had a full head of white hair. He said the couple seemed nervous. They thanked him and said a tow truck would arrive soon. As he walked back to his vehicle he noticed the man, in the truck, was now wearing sunglasses. It was late afternoon on a grey winter day. The man had his feet on the dash. He was wearing jeans and a denim jacket. Bern doesn't remember what he wore on his feet, but thinks it was boots. I think that is strange, because I can't remember what Elvis wore on his feet, and yet I too feel that he wore boots.

Out of curiosity Bern knocked on the window. The young man leaned over and rolled down the window. Bern said, "Hey, how you doin'?"

He replied, "I'll be a lot better when this d _ _ _ truck is fixed. I can't stand this cold weather."

Bern noticed a thick southern accent. He told the young man that he sounded like he was from the south. He said, "Yeh, see ya," and rolled the window up.

Bern drove on. However, he became very curious, so he pulled over again. He parked so he could still see the truck. The tow truck arrived, and in about ten minutes the repair was made. Bern followed the truck until it pulled into the drive-way of an old farm house. He turned into the next driveway that was about one-fourth mile farther. He wasn't going to be satisfied until he had talked with the young man with the southern accent.

The couple came to the door. He thought they were going to ask him to leave, but the young man came out of another room wearing a thick white terry cloth robe and slippers. Bern was surprised that this had happened within what he thought was five minutes. The young man asked the couple to let Bern in. Bern sat in a chair directly across from him, and noticed he was still wearing sunglasses. The young man said, "You know who I am?" Bern felt like his heart was beating a million times a second. The strange thing is that Bern didn't know who he was, so he didn't pick up on the voice as I did.

Bern replied, "You sound like someone familiar, and you kind of look like the person I'm thinking of." Bern felt fear. He honestly thought he may not be able to leave alive.

The young man leaned forward in his chair and said, "Who do you think I am?" Bern told him he could pass for Elvis.

In a most serious tone the young man said, "Elvis is dead." He then asked Bern what his name was and where he was from. He also asked if Bern knew Elvis had a twin brother who died at birth. Bern replied that he thought he had heard that, but he didn't know his name. He was told it was, Jesse.

The young man asked Bern the date of his birthday. He then walked out of the room and returned with a book. He sat down and pushed up his sunglasses, and then removed them. He paged through the book. Bern stayed a half hour listening to him quote things from the book. Bern doesn't say how it came about that he left. Did Bern say he had to leave or did the young man say something, so that Bern knew he was to leave? Bern walked to the door, turned, and asked, "Are you him?"

The young man...once again said, "Elvis is dead, but would you please not tell anyone what happened this day?"

Bern asked if he could visit again, and if he should phone first. He was told there was no phone; he found out later there was. Bern didn't want to be a pest, so he waited a week to return. The farm house was vacant.

After that Bern didn't keep his promise to the young man. He told someone about his experience, who told someone else, which resulted in Bern being interviewed by a DJ from Shreveport, LA. He didn't reveal everything that he discussed with the young man, and one of the things he must not have revealed was the location it happened.

Bern felt bad that the young man left without saying anything to him. He had a difficult time getting the incident out of his mind. He thought about it every day, and always wondered if it was Elvis.

Then late one night Bern received a phone call. It was a year from the day that Bern stopped to assist the people standing by the truck. After talking for twenty minutes he knew without a doubt that he was speaking to Elvis; the man most people thought was dead.

A friendship started that night that thrived to 2001. What has happened since the book was published is unknown to me. Bern could have died, but I am confident that if he is still alive, he and Elvis remain great friends.

Bern says Elvis knew he would need this small group of friends after his closest comrades began to disappear. He goes on to say they are all compatible in Elvis's numerology chart, which he totally believes in. Bern is telling his story from memory... because at that time he didn't keep a diary.

Bern testifies that Dr. Hinton's book is the truth. He says he believes that most people will believe what is said in the book after they read it.

Also included is a letter dated, January 17, 2001, from Linda Felix-Johnson. She says she is one of the small group of friends. She may be the Shuma who Elvis talks about in the book. However, I am not sure about this. She says she hopes the book will help readers understand why Elvis Presley had to leave this world as Elvis, and return to a more spiritual world as Jesse.

She says Elvis was born to sing and to entertain, but could not continue with the lifestyle he was leading. He changed the world of music and song forever. As Jesse, he lived as he desperately needed to. He is gentle, caring, and a spirit filled man, without fame and wealth.

She says the years of helping to care for him have been challenging and stressful. This is a lie because it is now known that she was not in the small group that helped him. She made an effort to pass herself off as another Linda. And she adds; for such a small group of individuals to keep a secret for so long is, in itself, a miracle.

Linda says that Dr. Hinton is one of her best friends, and that her respect for him is endless. She says it will take time for her to get back to being her. She became somewhat reclusive, and when Dr. Hinton's book was published, she looked forward to spending time again with her family and close friends.

She closes her letter with one of her favorite scriptures, 'All things work together for God to them that love God." She then writes, God bless you Jesse.

The last letter is dated January 18, 200l, and is written by TJ (Mr. C). Elvis mentions Mr. C. in his book, but I still don't have it figured out who he is, other than to know he is one of the small group of friends whom Elvis trusted.

He says TJ is the initials of his given name. He lives in a small Ohio town. He has known about Elvis/Jesse since 1989. It was Elvis, who called to tell him the Colonel had died. He hopes that people will understand why Elvis did what he did after they read the book written by Dr. Hinton. He says, "He was very sick, and I guess he just couldn't take being the King any longer." He goes on to say that he has one hundred plus letters written to him by Elvis that are kept in a bank safety deposit box. He was the guy Elvis asked to visit his cousin, David, in Michigan. He says the only reason he wanted them to meet was to share some great memories.

He wonders why God picked him from the millions of Elvis fans. He says it was a hot sunny day in 1989, when he, his ex-wife, two children, and some friends went looking for Jon Burrows. It seemed like everything fell into place, and they met, and that's when his story began. I wish he would have given us more detail. It would be nice to know where his search began and where it ended, and how long it took to meet Elvis. And where on earth did he get the idea in the first place. He must have been given a good clue, but by whom?

Mr. C. gives his testimony that everything Dr. Hinton writes in his book is true. He says he knows this because he is the one who introduced his dear friend to Elvis. He doesn't name the friend, but he says, over a period of time, she asked him if it was okay to tell the doctor about Elvis. Elvis gave his consent. This friend apparently is Shuma.

He goes on to say the reason the Dr. is writing the book is because, Elvis/Jesse wanted it that way. He says, "Please believe me, it's all true. I guess Elvis/Jesse thought it was time to set the record straight. If you are a true fan you know about the trash that was written about him through the years. What I wrote… please believe everything to be true."

He is wrong about one thing. I am a true Elvis fan, but I don't know about any trash that was written about him. I suppose it's because I haven't read the books. However, I did read some of the weekly tabloids when I saw something about Elvis on the front page. The only negative thing I remember is that some people made fun of his appearance. And I am betting many of those people who made fun of him have now packed on the pounds and look worse than he did. Is this where the, 'What goes around, comes around,' statement comes from?

He adds; Shuma is a gentle soul, and her husband, Sloan, is a gentle giant. The gentle giant was mentioned in the book, but I didn't know who it referred to…until now. A person learns a lot if they only keep reading.

The pieces of the puzzle finally fit together when he said, "If Bern hadn't trusted me, I wouldn't be in touch with Elvis/Jesse, and Dr. Hinton would not have written the book. However, I still don't know how Linda-Felix Johnson fits into the puzzle. She is the missing piece.

It's nice to know how these people came to know each other. It also gives me a warm fuzzy feeling knowing great friendships were developed with Elvis as the force behind it. Once again, Mr. C. asks the readers to believe that every word Dr. Hinton wrote is the truth.

Dr. Hinton says, "Fate will determine how this book will be judged, but absolutely everything that I have written is completely true. Jesse is alive and well. This is not the end... but the beginning."

So how was it judged? What happened after it was published?

Sometime last month, June 2010, I did a Google search. I don't remember what I asked, but I found some interesting information. And now I will share with you what happened, or at least, some of what happened.

I wanted to contact Dr. Hinton and Shuma. I was ready to share my story with them and I was confident after reading this book that surely Elvis/Jon/Jesse would be okay with my writing, *'Don't Cry Darlin'.'* I sent emails to two addresses I had for Dr. Hinton, and hoped he would reply. I didn't know Shuma's name, so I didn't know how to locate her.

Late one night, I was feeling sorry for myself. My 'thinker' changed gears. It had been in 'park' too long. I signed into EIN once again. Nothing had changed. I decided, 'Enough is enough.' I made a decision not to waste my time and brain power on something so meaningless. However, just before I signed out, I saw a posting from Shuma. Wow! One minute I got so excited and the next...will I just couldn't believe it. She said she wasn't going to be a part of the discussions any longer; mainly because of my reasons for not wanting to read the nonsense. She said she had already removed her email address and was starting her own website. I was totally disappointed because I so wanted to talk with her and now I couldn't because I didn't know her name.

A couple of days later I found a way to post a message. I simply said something like, 'Can anyone help me get in touch with Shuma? I have information that I know she would like to hear.' I left my name, email address, and phone number.

Two days later I received an email from the owner of EIN. He said he noticed my post and cautioned me about including my phone number and name. He thought I could be unnecessarily bothered by those who are regulars to the site. I told him I had thought of that and hoped to avoid it, but that it was important to me to talk with Shuma. I thanked him for his concern.

In the meantime I tried to contact her by other means. I wrote to her twice and lo and behold, instead of my emails going to her....they ended up in my inbox. I certainly wasn't computer savvy.

Five

Shuma

Golly! Shuma replied to my pleading. I am so very grateful to her, and I am so pleased to learn she is a really nice lady. Linda/Shuma welcomed me to her website. She was confident I would enjoy it; enjoy it I do. It is jam-packed with Elvis information.

A friend of hers saw my posting on EIN and relayed the information to her. I am grateful to her and am grateful to Shuma for going out of her comfort zone to give me the opportunity to visit with her. It didn't take us long to bond. I feel like I have known her for years, but it has only been nearly a year since we connected via email, so that makes us new friends. I am confident we will stay in contact until one of us moves on to bigger and better things, and by then I hope we can say we are old friends.

Anyone who has an interest in learning the truth about Elvis will be well rewarded by reading what she has posted on her website; lindahoodsigmontruth.com. Her site is provided absolutely free. There are no advertisements and absolutely nothing to sell. Linda asks her readers to digest what she writes and make up your own mind whether you believe it or not. "Everything on my site is the truth...plain and simple." She vows that there will never be one cent made off of her site or her friendship with Elvis/Jesse Presley. She states her website is in existence with the permission, approval, and one hundred percent support of Elvis…. who is now Jesse. Linda/Shuma and Elvis/Jesse have been great friends for eighteen years. I am grateful that she is willing to share their friendship. For me it has truly been a blessing.

I learned that she hesitated to contact me because of her past experiences. She was bombarded with emails of 'friendship' and quickly betrayed by many. She has suffered so much verbal abuse simply because she says Elvis is alive and now using the name, Jesse; his twin who died at birth.

It seems to me if a person doesn't like her site they should not go there. She is not forcing anyone to believe her. She is simply sharing her knowledge of Elvis.

Mid-December 2010, Linda made a fantastic announcement. She decided to give Elvis and her readers a Christmas gift. She set up a message board so fans could send Christmas wishes to Elvis/Jesse. She didn't limit the length of our message and we could include pictures. Her only stipulation was that she would scan our messages and would not post any if they were not well wishes to Jesse. This was not a forum for hatefulness towards her.

As far as she knows there was only one publishing of the paperback book that Doctor Hinton wrote with Elvis/Jesse giving him the information. Jesse told her he wanted to include more in the book and he did not want it published until after he leaves this earth. She said the book was published in such a cheap fashion and if it had been properly published it would have been an all time best seller. I totally agree. She doesn't know how many copies were printed, because she removed herself from the situation when Dr. Hinton went to a vanity press to publish. She thinks ten thousand or fewer were published. How ridiculous is that? What was he thinking?

I wanted to know how the book was advertised. She said, to her knowledge, it was on Doctor Hinton's web site and he did radio interviews. Some of those appeared in newspaper articles. He also interviewed on Fox 8 news. In his interviews he said Elvis/Jesse would be making a public appearance sometime in 2002. This was clearly not true. It was so sad that his book was so mishandled...what a shame. I totally agree with her. It was mishandled and it was unfair to Elvis/Jesse and his fans.

I learned that Linda Felix-Johnson is not Shuma. Shuma is Linda Hood Sigmon, and she says Linda Felix-Johnson is Dr. Hinton's side-kick; whatever that means. Perhaps I will learn more on this. In any case, I don't know who started what, or when it started, but apparently there are some hard feelings because the book was published before Elvis died. She believes Dr. Hinton and the other Linda convinced Elvis to publish it in 2001. Elvis, at one time, liked the idea because it worked out to be a good time....according to numerology. Perhaps he changed his mind, and wanted to wait until he knew all the information was included. If this is the case, the doctor continued forward on his own time schedule without giving further consideration to Elvis.

Elvis was concerned that people would be disappointed in him once they knew the truth; but he had to tell it. I imagine it was quite a burden for him to bear. I believe he hoped the book would give everyone peace of mind once they digested it.

Another thing that disgruntled her is the way the book was handled. I totally agree and this explains why I am disappointed in the book. She says, "It is sad his wonderful book was so badly handled, published, and promoted, that very few took it seriously." She learned in December 2000, that Elvis had given Dr. Hinton permission to contact publishers and to publish it in 2001. At that time, she begged Dr. Hinton to get a literary agent and show the agent the proof that Elvis is alive, and then let the agent contact publishers to get a good contract. Unfortunately, Dr. Hinton chose a self-publishing company.

Somewhere along the way Dr. Hinton gave fans false hope by saying Elvis would 'come out' sometime in 2002. By this time Elvis had no intention of getting in front of the camera. He simply wanted his fans to know he had not physically died in 1977…and why he did what he did.

Linda believes the combination of self-publishing and the false hopes given that Elvis would come out in 2002, destined the book for failure. She believes these two choices by Dr. Hinton created a stigma that overshadows the book to this day.

Prior to the release of the book, Elvis was attempting to prove his existence in a private way. Suzanne Stratford, a reporter with FOX 8, in Cleveland, Ohio, was chosen to be the most prominent media contact. Elvis had begun communicating directly with her. He wanted to arrange a private meeting without a camera crew. He asked if she and FOX could guarantee his safety. This interview would have been done in a secret location, and interviewing would be done… possibly without showing his face. Since Suzanne would see his face…she would have been a witness to the truth that it was Elvis she interviewed. However, without showing his face would people have believed it or would they think Suzanne wasn't credible? It appears we will never know. This is exactly the way I knew it could be done…and I thought it would be.

Gads! Why can't some people simply make it simple? I imagine some want to cause hurt and confusion, and some will try anything to get in the 'limelight.'

I about flipped when she said there was a written document, from FOX, which was to have been delivered to Elvis, through Dr. Hinton. The contract was intercepted, and never reached either of them. Someone on Dr. Hinton's end had confiscated it for their own selfish purpose. It was not discovered until much later; after it was too late. The same person who intercepted the document told Elvis lies about Suzanne. So he lost contact with her, and the historical interview never took place.

She sent an email to Suzanne that explained the situation. Since Suzanne didn't know her, she met with Dr. Hinton and Linda Felix-Johnson; they won her over. Of course, after the fact, Suzanne realized the truth of the matter.

During that time, she sent a tape of the FOX 8, Dr. Hinton interview to Elvis in May 2002. She wanted Elvis to know what was being said and shown. He replied with a letter that she received July 06, 2002. He expressed his disapproval of what Dr. Hinton was doing. He made it perfectly clear he had no intention of making himself public. He was not a happy camper that the doctor would think he would. She emailed Dr. Hinton and Linda telling them that Elvis asked for them to stop telling the fans they would be seeing him soon. However, they apparently continued giving 'false hope' throughout the year. She thinks they thought it would force Elvis to come out. I can't imagine anyone, thinking they could do anything that would force Elvis to do something he didn't want to do.

All of us are so blessed that he even considered writing a book to explain to his friends, family, and fans why he did what he did. She asks this question, "Could anyone keep their sanity, when being inundated with clamoring, worshiping, fans twenty-four-seven, for all of your adult life? Not to mention the mean spirited, demanding media, the death threats, the extortion attempts, the betrayal by lifelong associates, betrayal by even his family, and even losing daily contact with Lisa. She says that Elvis was under the stress of enormous demands, placed upon him by people who thought he was super-human. I'll let you ponder this thought.

Dr. Hinton solves the incorrect spelling of Elvis's middle name on the Graceland tombstone. He said it was Elvis who chose to do that. It was a clue that he was still alive. Even though he used both spellings, the extra 'A' in Aaron means alive. It's as simple as that.

Dr. Hinton says Elvis does not believe what he did in 1977 is a lie, because in his mind it was necessary. Shuma mentions death threats and extortion attempts. I don't remember any information about this in the book.

It appears what upset her so much is that Dr. Hinton began bragging a bit. She didn't use the term brag, but I am. He said,

"Elvis is ready to reclaim the limelight. There is part of him that wants his fans to know the truth. He has to start talking about his life as Jesse, and letting the fans know the truth."

I believe it was an interview with FOX 8 that he said the book was just the beginning. Shuma shared a tape of the interview. Dr. Hinton says, "This is just the tip of the iceberg of what's coming. Beginning next month, after his birthday, there will be a TV special where celebrities, who are his friends, who know this is true, will come forward. All of this will roll into the twenty-fifth anniversary in August." This would have been August of 2002. Perhaps you know if this took place. It doesn't seem to me that it did, because once again, why wouldn't everyone accept the fact that Elvis did not die in 1977? Apparently, this did not happen.

There is a rift among some of Elvis's long time and loyal friends. I'm sure he wouldn't want them to attack each other. I pray they will forgive each other for any wrong doing that another one took offense to. It seems to me each of them has stated, at one time or another, that it was extremely difficult to keep the Elvis story a secret for so long, but they handled it well. They should be grateful they had such a fantastic experience in their lifetime. I certainly am grateful for mine, even though it was nothing like theirs.

I have finally learned how Linda Felix-Johnson fits into the puzzle; so now it is complete. She is among the inner circle of Elvis's friends because she is a neighbor and former co-worker of Dr. Hinton. Her Uncle was, at one time, Elvis's dentist. Linda says the book was not released by a major publishing house because Elvis wanted to keep his book affordable. He also didn't want it to be sensational or trashy. Gads! Of course it wouldn't be trashy, but sensational? I don't get it. For people all over the world to learn that Elvis was still alive is sensational news, and the book should have been advertised so there would be no one who wouldn't hear about it. That's why I feel cheated. And I imagine there are many others who didn't hear about it also. In fact, this may be the first time some people learn about the book Elvis made possible. Linda Felix-Johnson said the larger publishers wouldn't have accepted the work, unless they saw Elvis type it. I imagine she is right.

How stupid would this be? There is so much evidence in the items Elvis sent as gifts; things that he owned for a long time. I hope the mailing wrappers were saved, or some people would say it's not proof because you might have come by them without Elvis giving them to you. However, most all the gifts were mentioned in their letters from Elvis.

He went to great lengths to document the gifts he sent. I'm sure he would think no one could question the gold tooth and hair samples. He knew he would need to provide his DNA. It is preposterous for anyone to require the proof they want. One would have to subdue or kidnap him, and carry him in front of the cameras. That's absolutely ludicrous. Why would anyone expect him to be treated like that?

Dr. Hinton and Linda Felix-Johnson say Elvis is a changed man, and that he is a very spiritual man. It's a completely different world for him. He's turned off by money and show business. Privacy is very important to him.

From everything I have read he has always been a spiritual man. He wasn't perfect, but he came close. His Mama taught him well. He had a heart full of spirit when he was just a young boy. When we listened to him sing gospel we could feel the essence of his spirituality. I hope to the end of his life, his health allows him to continue his love for learning and studying.

I hope he keeps his whimsical personality, and is grateful to know that by sharing his younger years with us, he made us all want more. By now he knows he has zillions of fans who still love him, and I believe he will throughout many generations. He has left a legacy like no one else. And in my opinion, nothing will ever change that.

Dr. Hinton says Elvis is more protected than the President of the United States, but he still doesn't trust all the people around him. This is so sad, because it adds unnecessary stress for all of them. It reminds me of his song, 'Suspicious Minds,' and it's not healthy to live in a suspicious environment. Hopefully, he will get past this and his people will understand why he has a difficult time trusting. Perhaps if they put forth extra effort to serve him he won't question their loyalty and trust.

When 'The Truth About Elvis Aron Presley, In His Own Words,' was published, Dr. Hinton was accused of using fraudulent information for the book. Elvis came to his defense. He sent a letter to the Attorney General of Missouri, who had the letter examined by a graphologist, who clarified the writer of the letter was indeed, Elvis Presley. Dr. Hinton was cleared of all charges of fraud. His practice is still doing well, and the only way the book has affected his practice is that it has caused a lot of stress. He hears from people all over the world, and says about ninety-nine percent of it is positive. I wonder how he gets any work done.

Mid-December 2010, Linda Hood Sigmon (Shuma) made a fantastic announcement. She decided to give Elvis and her readers a Christmas gift. She set up a message board so fans could send Christmas wishes to Elvis/Jesse. She did not limit the length of our message and we could include pictures. Her only stipulation was that she would scan our messages and would not post any if they were not well wishes to Jesse. This was not a forum for hatefulness towards her.

It was the best gift I could have ever received. I had been troubled for years at the way I acted when Elvis/Jon and I met, and I hoped to find out about the laughter when he and his entourage drove out of the parking lot. I also hoped to find out if he placed the ad in the newspaper, and if he and his 'bodyguards' saw me at the Dimond Mall.

Linda kept the message board up so we could also send New Year's and Birthday greetings, and then she shut it down. It was fun reading what everyone said, and she told us Jesse sincerely appreciated our words of love and concern. He also said he would not be answering any messages, because if he did it for one he would feel he should do it for all....and of course he couldn't do that. I wasn't disappointed....I was happy I had the blessing of sharing my thoughts knowing he would read them.

But there was one that I wanted him to answer. After the message board was removed Linda informed us that Jesse did reply to one of them, and it was the one I hoped he would answer. I don't remember the details, but it was sent by a female who had terminal cancer. I know hearing personally from him made her heart sing and I imagine it eased the pain of her final days.

If I remember correctly I wrote four times. I didn't know it would be therapeutic, but it was. By February my mind felt totally at peace. I felt like I had the closure that I so desperately needed.

Wouldn't you know it....often times there is one person who goes against the grain....so to speak. Linda made it quite clear her message board was not to be used to attack her; it was to be used only by fans who wanted to send loving messages to Jesse. There may have been some that she received that she did not post without anyone knowing, but she did post several from the same person. It seems like she told us why she wasn't deleting them, but I don't remember what she said. Perhaps she wanted Jesse to know what was being said because this person was a member of the 'Memphis Mafia' at one time, or perhaps she wanted her readers to know the guy is a first class Jerk. In any case, he has a potty mouth and a mean disposition. There is no way he will believe Elvis is alive... now living as Jesse. I believe he called Jesse a moron for saying he is Elvis. He thinks Jesse, Linda, and Dr. Hinton are phonies and frauds and that they owe Elvis fans an apology. He thinks

Jesse is conning Linda or Linda is conning her readers. This is preposterous. One day he told Linda he was there when Elvis died, and I believe it was the very next day that he told her he wasn't in Memphis August 16, 1977. Talk about confusion. How could anyone forget where they were that day?

He knows Elvis died in 1977. I know he was living April 12, 1988. I am positive he is still alive today and stays in contact with Linda. Do yourself a favor and read her site.

After seeing the picture of Elvis/Jesse with his grandson, Benjamin, this former member of the Memphis Mafia is totally disgusted. He says Elvis had plastic surgery some time in his early twenties, and the year before his alleged death. Because Elvis cared then about his looks....he certainly wouldn't let himself look like the picture. Doesn't he realize there is a big difference in minor surgery when you aren't trying to change who you look like opposed to major surgery where you want to change your looks so you won't be recognized? His lack of common sense is just ignorant. No pun intended. In any case...shame on him. Since he believes Jesse is a fraud and Elvis is dead, and can't defend himself....he will defend him.

I knew of this person before reading his irritating messages that were all directed at Linda. His name was recognizable as being an Elvis employee at one time. After reading his comments I think he should crawl under a rock. Maybe I'm a bit harsh, but how can he make such a spectacle of himself so openly? I actually feel sorry for him. I think he has acted childish. More than that, it appears to me he isn't intelligent enough to know that Elvis had to keep his inner circle very small in order for his plan to work.

It's now quite clear why Linda doesn't have an open message board. If she did it would probably be the same as the EIN message board. Linda's website shows class. I want it to stay that way.

For two years Linda continues to have problems with someone attacking her and her website. It causes so much extra work for her, and she has chronic pain from Fibromyalgia, and another painful situation. She certainly does not need the aggravation, and her readers don't need the stress of worrying that her website will be demolished. It doesn't seem possible that anyone would do such a thing. However it nearly happened just recently. I am going to share this event, so you will be aware that there are people like this that really need to be prayed for.

A major problem began for her late June. Linda's readers' couldn't get into her website. After contacting her server, Tip Top, she learned they failed to renew her domain name which she had contracted to do automatically, and "*coincidentally*" someone else was just waiting to buy it. It was strange that someone would want her name, and it was stranger that Tip Top would sell anyone's personal name to someone else to use.

Unfortunately her prominence on the Internet searches is totally out of her control. She earned her prominence in the search sites due to the number of visits to her site as compared with other sites which contained her name. This caused searches for her name to bring up the old results at the top of the list of results... which direct people to her old domain name, and when they click on those links, they get "site not found" which makes it appear that her site has been closed. It has been a mess for her readers as well as Linda. I imagine the guilty culprit is laughing at his accomplishment.

When Linda contacted Tip Top she didn't get much encouragement. Other than they will get her new domain name on Google, but that it will take weeks because Google is slow updating 'new sites.'

It's a shame this could happen or that it was allowed to happen. It took Linda over two years to accumulate over 119,000 visits, and to get back to the prominence on the

Internet which she held before this sabotage, she is told she will have to accumulate many thousands of visits again.

Soon after it was 'stolen' it was learned the thief was using it in a fraudulent manner. Linda was concerned readers would think it was her doing this, however anyone who knows her, and how she runs her website would know this honest, kind, and loving lady would never do such a despicable thing; someone new to her website might.

Linda asked Tip Top to give her the name of the person who now was using her old domain name. She had recently paid Tip Top over one hundred dollars to promote her website aggressively, and they were, but it did her no good when Tip Top had sold it to this 'thief'. Since she had to change her domain name she believed Tip Top should promote the new domain name just as aggressively; at no charge. Her readers agreed.

She told Tip Top, "God only knows what this jerk plans to do with the Email addresses and shipping information that they obtain from people while using my name!"

She says, "My site is the truth and the truth will never change. That is why I persevere to keep my site up despite repeated attacks."

Finally, Friday, July 8, 2011 someone came forward and bragged they had attacked the lindahoodsigmontruth.com website, and they would do so again and again and again until she had totally disappeared. They call themselves 'Presley Fan,' and were having a conversation with someone who was defending Linda's site. They were on another website.

Here is part of the quoted text:

"Just because one 'uses', and can utilize a forum that's been established for public use does not give them the right, as you say, to "rip into" anyone and call them names."

"Yes, it does; especially when the idea that Elvis is still alive, and has chosen the mentally retarded LHS to tell his story to is just so STUPID; like you."

"And, who are 'you' to speak up for 'others' when you say the "rest of us "?

"I am an 'Elvis fan,' for many years, and I hate freaks like you and LHS that spread this stupid, stupid, stupid lie. I will be there at every turn to bother and harass you, so get used to it."

"You would assume everyone here is a Judge Judy, or Judge Mathis wanna be."

"Actually, i assume that most people here aren't stupid enough to believe that Elvis is alive, and lives as that old guy who looks nothing like Elvis."

"And, since people should see and hear both sides before making up their own minds."

"No, dear, YOUR side deserves no respect. You are scum, filth, fraudulent; deserving a painful death. You are ruining the great legacy of Elvis Presley; only you're too dimwitted to even notice or care."

"I am just gonna post on Linda's new website again."

"And I'm just gonna attack it with a spam link again. That's right, loser. It was ME! Better tell LHS to get her site security up and working again. No matter though; I'll defeat it again, and again, and again, and again. Elvis Presley is dead. End of story: no debate. You are wrong, foolish, foolish woman. You can't even see just how stupid you are....taking the word of a woman you've never even met; a woman who has never even met that old guy pretending to be Elvis!

You're the perfect candidate for one of those UFO cults; where the head con-man leads his followers to death. I hope that happens with LHS and each and every one of you stinking, filthy, dirty, rotten, alivers'.

Gotta hand it to Jesse, though; He must be laughing his a_ _ off at how he's fooled LHS, and subsequently, idiots like you. Elvis Presley is dead."

As it turned out the person who admitted to shutting down her website was only bragging about his powers; he had nothing to do with it.

After a legal investigation was done it was determined that it was done for money, but it backfired on the perpetrator because Linda got her domain name back. It amazes me there are people who find pleasure in doing things that will cause her stress.

Here are a few quotes. Some are enlightening, and truly make a person think…And that is a good thing.

'When two opposite points of view are expressed with equal intensity, the truth does not necessarily lie exactly halfway between them. It is possible for one side to be simply wrong.' Richard Dawkins

'To speak the truth is a painful thing. To be forced to tell lies is much worse.' Oscar Wilde

'Beware of the half truth. You may have gotten hold of the wrong half.' Author Unknown

'Truth and Honesty is the oldest and most powerful of all of the human values.' Gary King

'No legacy is so rich as Honesty.' William Shakespeare

'There is none so blind as he who will not see.' Unknown

'Truth is like the sun. You can shut it out for a time, but it ain't goin' away.' Elvis Presley.

Wouldn't you like to know what he's thinking?

The Elvis Presley Eyes

Elvis does not read music. However, he has excellent ear tone.
He's playing 'Love Me Tender.'

The look I love.

Such a beautiful face....The Lord sure put him together nice.

Charisma....Charisma....Charisma

He's a hunk a hunk a hunk a man!

Six

Hmmm!

There are numerous reports regarding Elvis's reported death. I imagine they would make an interesting read. In any case, if anyone would spend the time doing the research for it I have the perfect title; *Hmmm!*

The television program, 20/20, did an investigation into the circumstances surrounding the alleged death of Elvis. I believe it was sometime in 1981. The investigative report was very convincing that Elvis did not die in 1977. Hmmm!

About two weeks after the airing of 20/20 the singer, Orion, disappeared. Hmmm!

Gail Brewer-Giorgio wrote a fictional book in February 1989. The title is '*Orion.*' It is an amazing story about a legendary performer who had several identities. The book was recalled by the publisher which was associated with the William Morris Agency. Overnight it disappeared from shelves across the country. I was fortunate to buy it before it was pulled. Incidentally, the William Morris Agency is the same agency that represented Elvis. Hmmm!

A singer named, Jimmy Ellis, was professionally known as 'Orion.' His natural speaking and singing voice sounded 'almost' like Elvis. Jimmy began his recording career in 1964. Shortly after Elvis's death, a masked singer by the name of 'Orion' emerged on the scene. He was big like Elvis, and he sang just like Elvis. Because of the mask, no one could tell his true identity. One fan described seeing 'Orion' from near the stage. She claims that 'Orion' left the stage between songs, and when he appeared moments later the sweat was gone from his armpits and back and she thought that his costume looked slightly different. After the song he left the stage, and the original 'Orion' returned. Hmmm!

Orion distributed, 'Farewell to the King' in 1989. Some of the words are, 'I died once. I had to be willing to give up everything…even the will to live.' It has been reported the last recording session at Graceland was, 'The Last Farewell.' Hmmm!

Neighbors' and many fans' reported never seeing digging of Graves at Graceland. Hmmm!

Another fan described how she rushed into a tour bus at an 'Orion show' and saw two Orion's' in the back of the bus. One ducked into the bathroom before she could get a good look at him, but he appeared to look like Elvis Presley. Hmmm!

I had never thought about what actually took place during an autopsy, so when I read what was reported my tummy was very queasy. Every organ, inch of tissue, and fluid samples was dissected and analyzed by several of the top experts in the country. The autopsy report cannot be obtained until 2027 because the family requested the autopsy instead of the court. Hmmm!

If the autopsy took place as reported how would it be possible to have the casket open? Hmmm!

It was reported his stomach contents were destroyed prior to the autopsy. Hmmm!

Two days before his alleged death Elvis telephoned a friend who reminded him of his mama. He told Miss Foster that he wasn't planning on going on the upcoming tour. She asked him if he had canceled it. He replied that he had not. Then she asked if he was ill. He told her he wasn't. He then told her not to ask any more questions and not to discuss their conversation with anyone. He said, "Don't believe anything you read. All of my troubles will soon be over. I will call you in a few weeks." Apparently... she did discuss their conversation. According to the author of *'Elvis Where Are You?'*....Steven Chanzes, a polygraph test proves she is telling the truth. Hmmm!

The day after Elvis's alleged death Lucy de Barbin received a single rose in the mail. The card indicated that the flower was from 'El Lancelot.' This was her pet name for Elvis, and it was unknown to anyone else. I'm confident this was Elvis's way of letting her know that he was not dead. It might have been better for Lucy if he had asked for it to be delivered a few days later. Hmmm!

Everyone involved with guarding him told a different story about what happened the day of his alleged death. And the stories have changed... and changed... and changed. At the time of Elvis's reported death it was said he died of a heart attack, drug overdose, suicide, murder, suffocation, a fatal karate chop to the neck, cancer of the bone marrow, poison, and natural causes. X-rays showed the body had no broken bones. Hmmm!

This same nurse said when she was told it was Elvis she didn't believe it. It was clear the body was not him. Hmmm!

It is said that Elvis's most prized possessions are a few of his books. He had a favorite Bible, books on death, several pharmaceutical books, Autobiography of a Yogi and Cheiro's Book of Numbers. After his alleged death these books disappeared and their whereabouts is unknown. Also missing were specific pieces of jewelry, pictures, and pictures of his mother. Hmmm!

One of the 20/20 television programs that ran in 1979 was hosted by investigative reporter, Geraldo Rivera. He reported on the cover-up that surrounded Elvis's alleged death. He pointed out the police closed the case the very night of August 16, 1977. Geraldo said it was the worst medical investigation ever made in this century. He went on to say that no real medical effort had been made to determine the cause of death. There was never a coroner's inquest. All photographs taken at the death scene, the toxicology reports; supposedly prepared by the medical examiner, and the notes from the medical examiner's investigation, disappeared from the official files. Hmmm!

One Paramedic said Doctor Nick was giving Elvis CPR, yet one of the doctors' at the hospital said the body was in rigor so long that if they had survived the person would have been in a vegetative state. (Not to mention a grotesque shape) It's obvious it is not possible to give CPR to a rigor body. Rigor mortis occurs after death. And when the body was found at Graceland it was stated the knees were drawn tight to his chest, now does anyone believe that body could be given CPR? Hmmm!

The Paramedics did not recognize the body as being Elvis. Hmmm!

One of the most bewildering discoveries is that Elvis signed his death certificate. A recognized document examiner reports that he did. And it wasn't filed until sometime after his alleged death. Hmmm!

During the week of Elvis's daddy's funeral a visitor to Graceland raised the edge of the turf covering his grave. He was astonished to see the ground was covered with green grass; no dirt was seen nor was there a break in the soil nor was it sod. Perhaps this is why Gail asked Elvis when his father died. It's a bit strange that he replied, "I can't talk about that at all." He could have simply told her the date, but at that time he may still have been alive. Then she said, "He did die, right?" Elvis replied, "I can't comment on that one way or the other...." Part of the tape was inaudible. Hmmm!

A respiratory therapist nurse was called into the autopsy room. She reports that drugs were administered...but none for cardiac arrest. Everyone in the autopsy room was required to sign a paper stating they would not discuss what happened in that room. Hmmm!

It's hard to believe that Elvis is seventy-five years of age now. In my opinion, it's time we all show some respect, and let him have his privacy. He has done everything he possibly can to tell us what he did and why he did it. We should thank him, and not cause him any further stress. Apparently, not everyone shares my opinion.

Patrick Lacy is the author of 'Elvis Decoded.' I have his book, but I have not read it yet. He is so sure that Elvis died in 1977 that he said, "If Elvis did fake his death, it is a certainty that he would not ever reveal that to anyone, least of all Donald Hinton and Linda Hood Sigmon, and certainly not to Gail Brewer-Giorgio. No way. If Elvis faked his death, he would be hidden away forever, and would never reveal that he is alive to anyone."

I don't fault him for the way he believes. He just happens to be a person who needs to see Elvis before he believes he is alive, and he may not even believe it then, but DNA would certainly confirm it.

Patrick brings up the subject of fraud. He believes anyone who says they have seen Elvis alive after August 16, 1977, to be liars. He says, "If Elvis Presley was found to be alive his estate would implode under fraud lawsuits, and his family would be in the poor-house." He also thinks those of us who have seen Elvis, and know he did not die in August 1977, should not report it, because we are causing Elvis harm. For Pete's sake, Elvis wants the masses to know. There is not a doubt in my mind that the facts stated in Dr. Hinton's book are true. I don't know if Patrick has read the book, but if he has, he doesn't believe it.

Patrick sees no purpose for anyone to report their experience when they came in contact with Elvis. He says reporting it means nothing without proof. Perhaps there will be enough proof for him one day, but that is a decision only Elvis can make.

He also says that those of us who tell our stories make us look foolish, and also make Elvis look foolish. I don't feel foolish, and I'm betting Elvis doesn't either. He says by telling our stories, we are insulting Lisa Marie and her family.

I imagine none of us even thought about harming Lisa Marie. It is clear to us that she knows her daddy didn't die when it was reported that he did. I also imagine she would prefer that we not tell our stories, but she can hardly fault us for doing so; because it has been a blessing to have the experience. She knows we aren't lying, but she will probably continue her story until she knows the truth from her is important and necessary for her to tell. People, who believe that he died in 1977, will certainly be befuddled and amazed. However, after they get over the shock of such great news, I believe they will understand and wish him nothing but good wishes.

Patrick also believes that anyone who goes public, and states that they believe Elvis Presley is alive, are risking embarrassing their family and friends. I doubt any of my family and friends will be embarrassed. In any case, I can't say that I believe Elvis is alive, but I can say, I know he did not die in 1977, and that he was living March 12, 1988.

Fraud is a deception deliberately practiced in order to secure unfair or unlawful gain that result in injury to another person. A person is a fraud if he assumes a false pose, like an imposter; a person who makes deceitful pretenses; someone who leads you to believe something that is not true. Any act of deception carried out for unfair, undeserved and/or unlawful gain; the assumption of a false identity to such deceptive end.

This pretty much sums it up. Knowing this… it is true… Elvis is a fraud. However, I can't imagine anyone suing him or the Presley estate. What he did was not with the purpose of hurting anyone, or with the knowledge his action would create wealth. He gave his future serious thought, and chose the kind of life he would have. He knew what he was giving up, and that his life would never be the same.

The thought of being found out or seen, probably didn't even enter his mind. It just goes to show us the best laid plans are flawed. It's certain he did lead many to believe he was dead, when, in fact, he was not. However, I hope there isn't anyone who thinks they have been harmed by his actions…other than the grieving, and not being able to see him perform.

Elvis never meant to harm or hurt anyone. He had no clue what his death would create, and I'm sure… when he did… he too was amazed. It's sad that he had to let us think he had died before he would fully understand just how much he was loved.

Maybe in hindsight it would have been best if he would have simply announced he was giving his last concert, and that he would continue to record music for us. Remember, he had help in making such a drastic decision, and he had people who helped him get through it all. He did it his way. And besides, with several people threatening to kill him, perhaps that is the only way he could feel safe and know his family would no longer be in danger.

Elvis's dentist was interviewed after his reported death. He told an interesting story about a time when Elvis needed an old broken root tip removed. He said Elvis mentally psyched himself up when it was time to numb him. When he reached for the syringe, Elvis asked, "What's that?" The dentist told him it was used to numb him. Elvis said, "Well, just give me a minute." Then he went into a trance like state. A minute later he said, "Ok, I'm ready." The doctor reached for the syringe. Elvis told him it wouldn't be necessary. The dentist was quite hesitant to continue. Elvis told him to go ahead and if it bothered him he would tell him to stop. The dentist did the work and sewed him up. He said Elvis had not moved; not even blinked. When he told Elvis he was finished, Elvis said, "I never felt a thing." This shows that Elvis was extremely good at meditation.

When the dentist was asked when Elvis had his last appointment he said he treated him the night before his alleged death. And he was shocked to hear Elvis was dead. He said Elvis appeared to be in perfect health. When asked what procedures he did, he said the usual cleaning. He made no mention of removing his gold tooth. Perhaps he was sworn to secrecy or maybe he simply forgot to mention that procedure. I wish the interviewer had told him that he heard Elvis had a gold tooth removed, just to hear his response. But then, maybe he wasn't aware of it at that time.

Before his alleged death, accusations and reports about his drug abuse were blown out of proportion. This troubled Elvis and made him angry. He responded to the situation at a concert in September, 1974. His anger showed as he denounced the reports. The fans were shocked because they had never seen him angry.

Elvis used prescription drugs and perhaps he occasionally used narcotics. He over-medicated because of extreme pain, but he was not into 'party drugs.' He also over-medicated in order to function. His schedule was grueling and wrecked havoc on his body. It is amazing that he lived through the torment. I imagine many of the ones who spread rumors, in regards to the drugs, were abusing their body by using stronger drugs than prescription drugs.

Actually, Elvis is against the use of drugs. I imagine that is one of the reasons he worked as an agent in the Drug Enforcement Agency.

He is also an educated man. It has been said he would set in the hall and read a book while his friends partied in hotel rooms that he paid for. Some of these 'friends' helped spread lies about him. I imagine he got really tired of all of it. He wanted more for himself. In fact, he probably wanted more for his 'friends.'

Is it so difficult to understand that he wanted a change in his life? Is it so difficult to understand that he just might want to improve his life? He has the basic wants and needs that we all have at various crossroads in our life. He had lived in poverty. He experienced life as a multi-millionaire. Perhaps he wanted to live a quiet, simple, and peaceful life; somewhere in the middle. And perhaps he succeeded in finding exactly what he hoped for.

I imagine there are many stories that have never been told; stories that a person told a friend or a family member, and they thought it was simply a case of mistaken identity. I also imagine there are people who have lived with the stress caused by meeting and talking with Elvis.

Remember the store receipt and the package of gum? I thought it was so important that early morning when I carefully put it in my bottom drawer. However, when I moved, I remember seeing the items, and wondered why on earth I had them. At that moment my brain scrambled, and I put them in the trash. This is just one example of the way my brain has worked after my encounter with him.

I wish those rich billionaires in Arizona would finance a project. It would be fun to get all the people together who have actually seen and talked to Elvis after August 16, 1977. We would be required to take a lie detector test before we would be invited to participate. This would weed out the 'loonies,' who just want to hear the results. It seems to me our stories would be accepted as truth once we had passed the lie detector test.

I am amazed that Elvis has been able to live with a lie for so long. Lies will eat a person up until they can't think straight, and finally they are brought to the realization that they know they have to tell the truth. And not just because it's the right thing to do, but because you know it's the only way you can truly have peace of mind. I can identify with this, and there are probably lots of you who can too.

Elvis is sorry for what he did; he has apologized and explained; the rest is up to us. I forgive him for anything he thinks he needs to be forgiven for.

If there is any among you who will not accept the truth now then you probably never will. If you don't accept the evidence that Elvis has shared with us I feel sorry for you. I hope by now you know those who said they saw him dead, they found him dead, or they autopsied his body, lied because they were made to believe he was dead; or they were sworn to secrecy for the benefit of Elvis himself. But that was then.... and this is now. Several of you, in your search for the truth, unknowingly were lied to, and so you base your findings on lies. And now you are determined that he is dead.

It does amaze me that many people, professional people included, did what they were asked to do: cover up, deceit, lie, or whatever you want to call it. It is wonderful to live in a country that still gives us the freedom to speak openly even if we don't always agree. However, I am confident Elvis would not want anyone to do any name calling because of him.

Elvis has popped into my mind so often through the years. I have re-lived it many times and sometimes I wonder if it was a curse instead of a blessing. I imagine there have been sightings and possibly encounters, such as mine, that I haven't heard about. If so, I hope those people handled it a lot better than I did, but more importantly, I hope they haven't found it as difficult to live with as I have.

There have been times that I heard Lisa Marie, Priscilla, or someone else swear he died, August 16, 1977. I just smile and say, "Sure." In the early years I imagine Priscilla had to tell the lie to support the decision that was made in regards to that day in August, but it seems to me that after all these years the threat of harm to any of them by unknown persons to us would no longer be a threat. I imagine it has been difficult for them to keep it a secret for so long, but after a while perhaps it was second nature.

The one that truly amused me is when the self-proclaimed psychic, Sylvia Browne, answered a question from a young lady in the audience of the Montel Williams show. Sylvia is/ was a regular guest on Wednesdays. One afternoon she was asked, "Is Elvis dead?" She didn't wait a split second before she flipped her hand, and calmly said, "Of course he is. He's dead." She immediately looked away to answer another question. I yelled, "You are a fake, Sylvia. You are a fake. How can anyone believe anything you say in your books?" And then I started in on Montel; "Montel, how can anyone with your intelligence believe what she says? How can you share your show with her?"

And then, quite the opposite is heard. Sometime in 1996, Marty Lacker and Billy Smith were interviewed in England. A newspaper printed the interview. Some of what was said is: Elvis was still alive. Elvis told them he felt alone and unhappy. He wished he could live a 'normal' life. On the day he was reported to have died he left Graceland in the back of a black camper van. Elvis had met a man named Scott who was terminally ill with Cancer. Scott went to Graceland to beg Elvis to help his wife and children. Elvis probably didn't hesitate because it was his nature to help those in need. Elvis noticed Scott had some of his features; blue eyes, same jaw line, size, etc. Elvis paid for Scott's plastic surgery to become his double.

In 1988, Marty was on the Larry King Television show. Gail's first book about Elvis had been published. He verbally attacked her for asking, is Elvis alive? He accused Gail of exploiting Elvis's death. He left viewers' believing he had seen Elvis in the coffin. However, in the book he wrote with Patsy and Leslie Smith he says he did not attend the viewing or the funeral. Sometime after the 1996 interview he said he was misquoted.

Elvis comes to me in dreams once in a while, and each time it's always the same; he tells me he wants his fans to know he's still alive, and he has done everything he can to show us, but we just won't listen; we don't believe. He laughs and says, "I told you they wouldn't believe you, and now they won't even believe me."

When I wake up I can't help but laugh, because I know he has told us. I am wondering like Elvis; I wonder if we would believe even if he went on a show as popular as 'Oprah's.' I don't think so...I honestly don't. As much as his fans want him to be alive I doubt they would believe it was him. I know he's no longer the young Elvis, but I'm betting he's still a hunk.

This is old news, but perhaps you didn't hear that Elvis's daughter, Lisa Marie, agreed to sell eighty-five percent of his estate on December 17, 2004, to businessman Robert Sillerman. It is reported to be a one hundred million dollar deal. Wow! That's a bunch of cash. Sillerman will own Elvis's name and likeness, the rights to his photographs and revenue from his music and films, and will run Graceland; his Memphis home. Lisa Marie will retain possession of Graceland and many of Elvis's 'personal effects.'

Elvis has probably shook his head many a time at what he heard, read, and saw since 1977. However, he knows that those of us, who had the blessing of, 'up close and personal sightings,' know the answer to the question; did Elvis die August 16, 1977?

By now I am sure Elvis/Jon/Jesse, doesn't intend to make a public appearance. I imagine there was a time when he wanted to, but EPE (Elvis Presley Enterprises) quickly put the brakes on that by saying something like my grand-pappy would say, "You made your bed....now lie in it." At this point he may figure, what's the use? He has done so much to tell us and we still believe he is an imposter.

There was a time that I believed he would have a video made, with as much privacy as possible, so that when it was televised he would be somewhere in hiding so he couldn't be swarmed with fans and news media. That would be the end of the debate and the 'wondering.' Perhaps he has made one with instructions to televise it after he goes on to bigger and better things. Time will tell.

I hope he accomplished many of the things he couldn't accomplish as an entertainer. I'm just so very sorry that the events in his life turned out the way they did for him to think he had to do what he did. He has done a lot of good in his forty-two plus years. I am confident he will be given many blessings for his service and sacrifice. And I truly am sorry he didn't have a 'normal' life.

If Elvis has asked someone to write a second book after he has gone on to bigger and better things, it would be a great read. It would be special if he wanted us to know what he did all those years before he actually died, and how the secrecy was handled. If that book ever gets written, I would love to be here to read it.

Seven

Everybody Has A Story

In the last four months I have read forty-two books written about Elvis. I have another twenty-three yet to read, plus I would like to find five others that are very difficult to locate. I hesitated to order some of the books because several fans and Elvis thought the books were unflattering. I also read that Elvis was extremely concerned about the book that was published just a couple of weeks before he changed his lifestyle. I believe it was written by three of his bodyguards who were dismissed because it was costing him too much money paying their attorney fees. They used unnecessary force in their work, and had been counseled to control their behavior. Finally, Elvis or his daddy decided, 'enough is enough.' Because of that Elvis thought they were writing it to get back at him. They said they were simply trying to show Elvis he was a different Elvis.

After reading the book I imagine it was a little bit of both. Elvis worried about what his fans would think of him after they read the book. It is said he tried to pay the guys for not publishing it, but they weren't interested in the deal. I for one didn't think any less of him. I imagine there were some who thought he should be perfect, and expected him to be. But he is human; none of us are sinless, and many of us have dealt with habits that are detrimental to our mental, spiritual, and physical health. It's what we do about it that counts. I know

Elvis came to terms with his weakness, and got on the right path and stayed on it. This is what his fans should remember about him.

'*Elvis and Gladys,*' written by Elaine Dundy, was published in 1985, by McMillan Publishing Company, and in 2004, by University Press of Mississippi. I was disappointed in this book. I expected it to be a fun read; instead I thought it depressing. Of course, not everyone shares my opinion; imagine that. Someone from The Boston Globe said, "Nothing less than the best Elvis book yet." I don't know how many books were published prior to this one. However, I recently read that well over one thousand books have been written about Elvis. This book actually angered me. I had to walk away from it several times to calm my mind.

I believe none of us are perfect, and we are all unique. I think that's what makes each one of us interesting. I have very poor friends and I have very rich friends, and of course, I have many friends who have all that is needed, but have the desire to have more. I fall into this group. However, regardless of what group I was in I would still be kind to all. I feel comfortable whether I am dressed up or down; depending on the occasion. I don't belittle anyone nor do I make fun of anyone. And I don't remember ever doing so. It is so not necessary, and I believe that anyone who displays these actions is to be pitied.

There is so much said in this book that would make anyone angry or sad if it was being said about them. Some people really do believe they are more worthy than others.

A man was being interviewed or was simply asked what he thought about Elvis. His remarks were so disgusting that he made it clear he wanted to remain anonymous. I believe one question was, "How did Memphis society react to having Elvis in their midst?" He said he only had one overall impression about Elvis's position and acceptance in Memphis. "And that is naturally from the point of view of the world I was born and raised in....the world of the country club, etc." He said they thought of Elvis as an embarrassment to the community because they thought his art was tacky, common, vulgar, and lower-class. When his wealth and fame began to benefit Memphis charities he was referred to as a 'fine young man.' Even so, he was still secretly mocked as being vulgar and tasteless. He made the comment that people 'of that class' lacked culture. And even though Elvis was admired, we wouldn't want him to marry 'our daughters' or sit at 'our table,' or belong to 'our club.'

In my opinion, Elvis has more class in his little finger than this man has in his whole body. This man is entitled to his opinion, but it certainly is a disgraceful opinion. No wonder he wanted to remain anonymous. Elvis is probably used to turning the other cheek, but he is a sensitive guy filled with love for all people. So it had to be people who felt this way about him that caused him lots of hurt. I hope by now he has put it all behind him so that he is able to think 'happy thoughts' most of the time.

Before Elvis moved into Graceland he bought a beautiful house in a quality neighborhood. His mama didn't like being without close neighbors. It would have been perfect for her, but the neighbors weren't friendly, and she became very lonely and depressed. The neighbors didn't like the noise and all the traffic caused by Elvis moving into the neighborhood, and they objected to Gladys hanging laundry outside. She preferred the fresh smell opposed to the heat smell from being in an electric dryer. They drew up a petition hoping they could all buy his home. Elvis was irate and suggested that he buy their homes. When they learned Elvis's home was the only home in the area that was paid in full, and that he paid cash they were embarrassed; they dropped the proceeding. However, it was clear to Elvis his mama would never be happy there, so he told his parents to find a place where they would like to live. In a short time they found Graceland and he made it into a beautiful home. Elvis was happy that he was able to give his mama a home that she felt comfortable in. She could raise chickens, hang her laundry outside, and she could do anything she wanted. She didn't have close neighbors, but she could be proud of her home. Seventeen months later Gladys died at the age of either forty-two or forty-six. There appears to be a discrepancy in her age. The diagnosis was Hepatitis. Elvis was devastated. His Aunt said he was never the same Elvis after her death.

'*Elvis: A Biography,*' written by Jerry Hopkins, was published in 1972, by Warner Books, Inc. There are many biography's written about Elvis. I am glad I chose this one to read. It is a great Biography. Jerry fills it with an enormous amount of information about the extraordinary man; Elvis Presley.

'*If I Can Dream,*' written by Larry Geller was published in 1990, by Avon Books, by arrangement with Simon and Schuster. This is a personal chronicle from Elvis's spiritual advisor and friend. It's a very interesting read. I highly recommend it as a must read.

'*Elvis: The Last 24 Hours,*' Written by Albert Goldman, was published in 1991, by St. Martin's Press. This book was a waste of my $3.99. Everyone is entitled to their own opinion, and mine is he has absolutely no class. First of all his entire book was written without any personal experience with Elvis. He says most of his material was furnished by David Stanley, who is Elvis's stepbrother. It was difficult to get through the first few pages, but I continued to read every word he wrote. I was a bit angry and didn't like the way I felt as I read. It definitely is not a fun read. It leaves me saying, Albert Goldman is a very narrow minded person, and he has boldly shown his ignorance. He certainly shows the reader that a writer isn't naturally intelligent. He tells the reader that Elvis was a drug addict, never stood for anything, never fought a battle, never made a sacrifice, and never raised a finger to struggle on behalf of what he believed or claimed to believe.

Where on earth has Albert Goldman been all these years? It appears to me he has had his head in the sand. He goes on to say, "Even gospel, the music he cherished above all, he travestied and commercialized, and soft-soaped to the point where it became nauseating." He says that when Elvis sings a spiritual song he sounds insincere. It's a shame that Albert Goldman's heart is not in the right place. I so enjoy hearing Elvis sing gospel and I feel he bears his soul with every word he sings. The last sentence he writes is, "What you see at the end of Elvis's life is his fitful, but hopeless struggle to break free of his image; a struggle that he began too late, and with too little will to win. And he is so wrong about that. Basically, I suppose it's a case of 'consider the source,' except that I never heard of Albert Goldman until I read his book. He is a 'bestselling author.' However, that doesn't mean he knows what he's talking about.... because he doesn't.

After thinking about the total book; it seems to me Albert Goldman is jealous of Elvis. He set out to try to hurt him with the words he wrote. It wasn't necessary. There are lots of talented singers, actors, dancers, and musicians, and yet we all have our favorites; but we don't put down those we don't like. There's nothing wrong with saying, "I'm not a fan of the Beatles'. I simply don't like their music." And that's all that needs to be said. We are all different; none better than any other in the eyes of our Heavenly Father and Jesus. We each have a destiny, and it would be wise, while we have the opportunity, to make our journey showing more love for one another.

'Inside Graceland,' written by Nancy Rooks was published in 2005, by Xlibris Corporation. Nancy was Elvis's maid. This is a fun read.

'Elvis Undercover – Is He Alive and Coming Back?' written by Gail Giorgio, was published in 1999, by Bright Books. Gail is a fantastic writer. Her words flow with excitement and intrigue. It's a fun read. Gail certainly makes the reader want more. This book is copyrighted eleven years after my amazing encounter with Elvis.

Gail is a marvelous investigator. During her research she uncovered mountains of evidence that the general public was not intended to learn until Elvis wanted it known.

During her investigation she learned of a racketeering operation the Government was investigating. It involves racketeers who conned billions of dollars from unsuspecting citizens. Elvis was one of the citizens. The Government's file name is, 'Operation Fountain Pen.'

Elvis was a chief witness against the major criminal organization that was the subject of Operation Fountain Pen.'

He provided cover for a Federal agent in 1974. It's possible this was the beginning of an urgency to expedite his desire for a 'new' life. These files were not declassified until 1985. More than six hundred pages were still classified in 1994.

Gail has started a book titled, 'Operation Fountain Pen.' Watch for it; if it is ever published I encourage you to purchase it. It's certain to intrigue and excite the reader.

Gail received a phone call October 10, 1988, from someone who identified himself as Elvis. She was asked not to record the conversation, but she did and then included the lengthy conversation in, 'Elvis Undercover.' A cassette tape was also attached to the book. People removed the tape without buying the book so the tape was no longer included. There was no tape with the book I purchased, but I have listened to a few minutes of it, and it is definitely Elvis. Those people who took the tape without purchasing the book missed out because it is very interesting. When Gail taped his call that was most likely why he made a negative remark about her; he was a bit disgruntled.

Gail asked him if he had lost weight. He told her he had, but that he had gained it back. He felt more at peace with the added weight. He wouldn't have said that if he looked like he did on stage the later part of his performances, and I can understand he would not wish to be as thin as he was when he first began performing, so I imagine he looked the same as he looked when I saw him, six months earlier. He looked great. He didn't look like a skinny teen. But he wasn't overweight for his height and bone structure. It was obvious he had worked hard to accomplish such a magnificent look.

'I Called Him Babe: Elvis Presley's Nurse Remembers,' written by Marian J. Cocke, was published in 1979, and reprinted in 2009, by Marian. This is a sweet book; a loving and tender portrait of Elvis. Few people knew Elvis as she did. One day Elvis threw a sock on the bed that had a hole in it. Marian picked it up and darned the hole before she threw it in the trash. Elvis was a bit bewildered, so he asked her why she repaired the hole before trashing it. She told him she just wanted to be able to say she darned Elvis Presley's socks. You can purchase this book at epnurse@bellsouth.net.

'Elvis His Spiritual Journey,' written by Jess Stearn, was published in 1982, by The Donning Company Publisher's. It is also published under the names of 'Elvis' Search for God,' and 'The Truth About Elvis.' I was unaware of this. In fact, I didn't know it could be done. In my opinion, it's a bit unethical. I bought a copy of all three before I learned of the title change. Elvis wanted it written, and he wanted Jess to write it. Jess dedicates it to Elvis – Whose book it is. This is one of my favorite books about Elvis. I highly recommend it.

'Elvis Presley's Graceland Gates,' written by Harold Loyd, a first cousin of Elvis, was published in 1998, by Jimmy Velvet Publications. He tells of interesting happenings while he worked as a gate guard. I had never thought about the many stories that could be told about that location. I was never one of the fans milling around the gate. It was an interesting job for Harold, and he was grateful to Elvis for adding him to the staff in a time of great need.

'Return of the King: Elvis Presley's Great Comeback,' written by Gillian G. Gaar, was published in 2010, by Jawbone Press. This book covers the last ten years of Elvis's life. However, its main focus is the revival of his career starting with his 1968 NBC-TV 'Comeback Special' through to his return to live performances in Las Vegas a year later.

'*Leaves of Elvis' Garden: The Song of His Soul,*' written by Larry Geller, was published in 2007, by Bell Rock Publishing. This a touching read written with love. Larry is Elvis's spiritual adviser and close friend.

"*The Presley Arrangement,*' written by Monte Wayne Nicholson was published in 1987, by Vantage Press, Inc. This is the most intriguing story I have read about Elvis. It is absolutely fascinating. The author says it is a novel. I believe it is a non-fiction novel in the company of 'Roots,' written by Alex Haley and 'In Cold Blood,' written by Truman Capote. This book was copyrighted in 1987; one year before Gail Giorgio's book, 'Is Elvis Alive?' was published. Monte was a detective with the Los Angeles Sherriff's Department when he did extensive research on a reported sighting of Elvis on the grounds of Graceland....hours after his alleged death. I don't know how many copies were printed, but they disappeared from bookstores almost immediately. And they weren't all purchased by fans. The books simply were gone. I believe it was another case of a deliberate way to keep this amazing information from the general public. It is highly probable this is the reason the book is extremely difficult to find. And if you do locate it be prepared to pay a premium.

A recently retired LAPD cop clicks his camera on the grounds of Graceland. He was a veteran street cop, so he had worked his share of patrol, but he worked the last few years as a detective. When he retired he was gifted with an expensive Nikon camera with a telescopic lens. He and his wife were excited about going on a planned cross-country trip in their new camper. Their destination was Muncie, Indiana. He wanted to visit his brother, but he was going by way of 'Route 66.' He also wanted to visit a buddy who lived in Memphis and visit Graceland. When he vowed to take pictures of Elvis with his new camera his friends chuckled. He was a forty-eight year old Elvis freak. His wife thinks he acts like a teenage girl simply hearing the name 'Elvis.'

He was excited to finally be on Presley Boulevard. He quickly found a parking space and was on his way towards the mansion; leaving his wife to lock the camper. When she arrived at the front gate he wasn't there; he was just turning the corner; heading towards the back of Graceland. He thought it was more likely Elvis would be in the back yard rather than in full view of the fans at the front gate. As he started to climb up to get a better look he saw a person he thought was a body guard. He appeared to be walking the fence line. Just then the bodyguard placed his walkie-talkie to his ear, listened for a second, and then ran towards the mansion. He had a chance to get over the wall.

In the distance he heard a helicopter approaching the mansion. He was amazed that a helicopter patrolled the mansion. He hid behind some bushes. He was determined he was going to get a few pictures. As the helicopter descended three figures moved quickly towards him. He thought he had been discovered. Just as he was going to dash for the fence, he realized they hadn't noticed him...they ran right past him. That's easy to understand. They had their own agenda and why would they even give a thought to the fact that anyone would have scaled the wall at that exact time and in that same part of the estate? He was amazed; less than two hundred feet away stood Elvis. This was a chance in a lifetime. He ran towards Elvis, but he thought he was too late. The copter had landed, and it appeared Elvis was concentrating on getting on board. He yelled, "Hey Elvis." Upon hearing his name, without hesitation, Elvis stepped back and looked in Mark's direction. The Nikon clicked twice and he made a dash to the fence; scaling it immediately. He was excited, but very nervous. He heard the chopper rising, and when he looked behind him he was elated; no one was following him, but he continued to run. He was anxious to tell his wife about his amazing achievement.

In the meantime, she is standing at the front gate waiting for him to return. She hears an ambulance siren, the gates to the mansion open, and she quickly learns the ambulance is heading for the front door. Two Paramedics rushed to take a large wheeled stretcher from the back of the vehicle. They ran up the stairs, and into the mansion. She stepped onto the driveway to get a better look at what was happening. A horn from behind her startled her. She jumped back to the sidewalk just in time to avoid being hit by a large black limousine. The limo screeched to a halt behind the ambulance. An elderly man sprinted up the steps, and into the mansion. He carried a black bag, so he appeared to be a doctor. By now people were beginning to mill around the gate, and near the front door. She thought it was 'funny' how anything to do with Elvis attracted a crowd. Soon after, a police car arrived to keep what had developed into a large crowd out of the street. It seemed like an eternity before the stretcher would be removed from the mansion; someone was on it. The man she thought was a doctor was following close behind; He climbed into the ambulance. The doors were shut, and the ambulance moved ahead with siren blaring. A large white limo followed closely behind. The gates closed, and everything appeared 'normal' again. She headed towards the camper since her husband had not returned; he was there. They swapped stories, but her husband wasn't the least bit interested in what she told him. He was feeling quite smug on getting his pictures.

He pulled the camper into traffic and headed towards Indiana. There was too much static on the radio, so they listened to an eight track tape. (A thing of the past) She wanted to know what happened at Graceland, but she would have to wait.

It was a bit casual how they learned Elvis had died, and more than a little suspicious right from the beginning. During dinner conversation she suggested that he tell his brother about what happened at Graceland. They about choked when they heard the words; "dying wasn't it?" His first thought was the value of his pictures. He figured they were the last pictures of

Elvis alive. He asked when it happened, and knew something didn't compute. He took the pictures at two o'clock. Elvis was said to have died between eleven in the morning and one in the afternoon. How could anyone make such a mistake? She told them that someone else was ill at the Presley Mansion when they were there, and then proceeded to report what she saw.

Her husband, being the sleuth that he was, knew he had to return to Graceland; he had an investigation to do. He was an experienced pilot, so he rented a plane and returned to Memphis. On his return to Muncie he ran out of fuel. Both tanks emptied simultaneously. He had a safe landing, but it was discovered the fuel lines had been cut. Someone had tampered with the plane. He now had something else to investigate. He returned to Memphis, and while there two men approached him, and told him they represented someone who was interested in a picture he took August 16. They were prepared to pay five thousand dollars cash for it. He was told he had two days. What did they mean? He was determined to find out who would pay five thousand dollars for a picture. When he had the answer he would decide what to do with the pictures. When the film was picked up he realized he had two pictures. He gave one to his wife and kept one. He thought since the men thought he only had one he might keep the second one for 'insurance.' He also thought by waiting the offer might increase. In the meantime, while his wife was eating lunch two men approached her. They looked like the men her husband described. They had the cash. She had the picture, and the sale was completed. She thought she had done a good thing. However, he was irate. Since the buyers had their picture they would not be contacting him about the second one. There was nothing he could do....or was there?

He makes an exciting effort to unravel what is an intricate mystery. He fears for his life, and is concerned about the safety of his family. The excitement and intrigue will immediately hook you into not wanting to close the book until you read the last page.

Truth is stranger than fiction, and this is, without a doubt, 'a story so controversial it could only be told as fiction.' The plot twists and turns. This reads like a thriller; a contemporary thriller. It will keep you on the edge of your seat.

Surprisingly, he received another generous offer. He could write a book about his experience including everything he discovered during his investigation. He would be given a writer to help him since he had no prior experience at writing. He was guaranteed his book would be promoted to the best-seller list; no matter what the cost. He would receive all royalties. This was one of those things that, 'if it sounds too good to be true….it is.' He asked, "What's the catch?" He was told it would have to be written as fiction, and in the preface he was required to say he had made it all up. On the front cover, 'A Novel' is printed just below the name of the title and previous to Chapter one it states, 'All characters portrayed in this book, with the exception of Elvis, are fictional. Any similarity to actual places or events is purely coincidental.'

He gave it some serious thought before he said he would do it, but there was a condition. He wanted an interview with Elvis. He was told to go home, and wait for a call. Several days later he received the call; a meeting was scheduled. He could ask any question, but Elvis was not required to answer it. The length of the interview was not established. He would have to leave when he was told the interview was over. The complete interview is in the book. When he was told they had to leave he said, "Thanks, Mr. Presley, and good luck."

"You're welcome, sir. I hope we can end this now."

He told him he would follow their agreement."

Is this couple still living? Have they told their children about their experience the day Elvis was reported to have died?

The Presley Arrangement will add fuel to the fire for those who believe Elvis is alive. It is far more than entertaining. It is a testimony that Elvis was not in need of a casket on August 16, 1977.

Monte didn't publish his book until 1987. Is it no wonder that nearly ten years after Elvis was reported to have died that Elvis said, "I hope we can end this now?"

'Elvis, My Brother,' written by Billy Stanley, Elvis's half brother, was published in 1989; by St. Martin's Paperbacks. It too is a really good book. It shows a tremendous amount of love for Elvis. It shows Elvis is/was not perfect....but close to it. What I really like is that Billy showed how drugs can get to a person, and how hard it is to recover. I felt so sorry for Billy. It had to take a lot for him to share such personal stuff about himself. Just when I thought he was going to lick it.... there he goes again. I must have said, "oh Billy" three or four times. My heart went out to him. I almost went to the back of the book because I was anxious to know how it ended, but I was patient and lived through it with him. I am so pleased to learn he had two years in recovery when he finished writing. I so hope he has been strong enough not to go back to it. The one thing I liked so much was how the three brothers were close and stood by each other from the time they were young through adulthood. And how they stood by Elvis, and loved him dearly, and how Elvis treated them with love from the moment he was introduced to them. He was a wonderful big brother. Billy's story would be a great read for anyone who is currently experiencing a dependency to drugs.

'My Life with Elvis,' written by Becky Yancey and Clifford Linedecker, was published in 1977, by St. Martin's Press. Becky was Elvis's Private Secretary. This is a fun read, and I encourage you to read it.

Eight

Loving You, and You, and You, and You, and 'You'

'*Last Train to Memphis,*' written by Peter Guralnick was published in 1994, by Back Bay Books, and is a great read. It is actually volume one of a two volume Elvis biography. The second volume is titled, '*Careless Love,*' which I have not read. These books look great on my bookshelf. Placed together a picture of Elvis's face can be seen. I have never seen this before, and I think it is quite nice.

Peter has put together a fantastic biography. I previously thought, '*Elvis: A Biography,*' written by Jerry Hopkins was the only one I needed to read. However, I now believe Peter's work will be the definitive biography of Elvis. In this first volume is included a chapter titled, 'Without You.' It tells about Elvis's romance with Dixie Locke; his first 'crush.' But was she?

Dixie was fifteen and a sophomore at South Side High School at the time. It is said they met at a church function the later part of January 1954. Elvis was drawn to her church, 'The First Assembly of God,' because of his love of gospel music and the 'Blackwood Brother's quartet;' they played at the church regularly. I am not a member of this church, but I have several friends who are, and I have attended several times. Each time

I was deeply touched by the Holy Spirit. The music definitely contributed to the spirituality I felt.

Dixie liked Elvis the moment she saw him. I chuckled when I read she made sure Elvis overheard her make plans with a girlfriend to go roller-skating the following Saturday night. This is something I would have done if I would have been allowed such a freedom. My dad was extremely strict. Perhaps he was simply being over-protective. In any case, Elvis pulled through....he appeared at the roller dome. Dixie was supposed to go home after the first session, but Elvis invited her to go for a coke. He took her home well after the end of the second session; she was in love. Elvis told her he would call her the middle of the next week and make arrangements for the weekend. She was concerned when Elvis was not at church the next day, but later in the day he called. Yup! Young love had control. They went to a movie that night, and again on Wednesday. He gave her his ring a week from their roller-dome meeting; they were going steady.

Two weeks later Dixie met Elvis's folks. They became very close and Dixie's parents got along great with the Presley's. Dixie said Elvis's mama was one of the warmest, most wonderful, and genuine people she had ever met. They became great friends. Many times they had lengthy conversations whether Elvis was home or not. Almost immediately Elvis and Dixie were nearly inseparable.

One night, about a month after meeting, they separately went to an all-night gospel singing; sponsored by the Blackwood's. They were surprised to learn they had another common interest. Elvis shared his dream of becoming a singer with Dixie.

He went to work as a truck driver, and gave most of his salary to his Daddy. He kept enough for gas, and for the expense of dating. His free time was spent with Dixie.

That summer they went everywhere together; movies, all night gospel concerts, and even church. They would spend hours listening to music at the record shop where they could enjoy a soda at the fountain. It was quite a 'summer romance' that didn't end until October 1955.

It is said their relationship became passionate very fast, however they agreed they would save that special moment for when they got married.

He didn't want to drive a truck all of his life and he had no immediate possibilities in the field of music, so he decided to learn how to be an electrician.

They were separated for the first time the early part of July. Dixie went on a two weeks' vacation with her parents. They promised to be true, and to write to each other. Dixie reassured Elvis and herself that nothing would change; when she returned they would still have the rest of the summer ….they would still have their whole lives in front of them. This truly was young love. After seventy-six years' of living I don't think there's anything like it.

Late in the evening the Locke's were returning from their vacation. Dixie heard Elvis singing, 'Blue Moon of Kentucky.' Neither of them knew the magnitude of what would happen in the future. During 1954 and 1956 when his stardom began to rise he was adored by those who heard him, and by those who were lucky enough to see him perform.

Elvis told her to be at his house when he got home from work. For quite some time everything seemed to be the same between them. Once again they were nearly inseparable when Elvis wasn't working. Dixie had not yet turned sixteen at this time.

Elvis sang his heart out. He was doing exactly what he wanted to do. He was his own witness of his dream coming true. However, he couldn't know what was about to happen, and I imagine he was not prepared for it; the cheering, the adulation, and the humongous crowds. He was on his way; the journey of a lifetime….his lifetime.

Dixie worried about Elvis when he was away even though he called her often to express his undying love. She prayed for his success, and she prayed his success wouldn't change him. When he was home she worried because things were changing. Three months earlier the main thing on their minds was marriage, and whether they would have the strength to wait. Now Dixie thought his mind was somewhere else. He was distracted; wherever he was he was recognized. He was becoming a hometown celebrity, and he didn't know how to act.

Dixie and Elvis's mama shared their pride in the direction Elvis's life had taken, but they also consoled each other over what they had lost.

Early in their relationship Elvis played small concerts and clubs. He was excited, but he thought it was a case of 'hometown boy makes good.' Dixie said Elvis was still totally innocent and spontaneous; he wasn't prideful, and he wasn't conceited. They dated steadily from early 1953 until October 1955.

Elvis escorted Dixie to her junior prom at South Side High School. He graduated at Humes High in 1953. She was proud to show him off to her friends, but she found it difficult to fit in with his friends. Some of the new guys that were hanging around were not the kind of people they had ever been drawn to. They used horrible language and they had the dirty smoking habit. It was a group of people she felt totally uncomfortable with.

Around this time Elvis seemed to come alive only when other people were around. He seemed to crave their attention.

They had argued more than once to the point of breaking up. Dixie would give back his ring or he would ask for it. The arguments were always about the same thing; where was she when she wasn't home when he called? What was she doing while he was away? Who was she seeing? He couldn't stand for her to have any kind of independent existence. He was very jealous and possessive. Dixie kept her promise to Elvis to remain his girl, but she was sure Elvis knew he was being unreasonable, but he simply couldn't help this type of behavior. Their breakups only lasted a day or night and sometimes times he would drive around the block, and they would sit on the porch and cry. They didn't really want to break up; they were friends, and they loved each other.

Dixie continued spending lots of time with the Presley's. Often times she spent the night with them and slept in Elvis's bed when he was gone. She and Elvis's mama often cooked together, ate and shopped together, and sometimes go out for a walk. They were a comfort to each other, and made an effort to console each other. The Presley's resisted the lifestyle Elvis was getting into, but they had lost control of him. In a year he would be the legal age to make his own decisions.

August 15, 1955, Elvis proudly signed his signature at the top of a document that named Colonel Tom Parker as his special advisor.

Elvis's success snowballed very quickly. He was constantly performing and creating a humongous fan base. He and Dixie slowly drifted apart. He was consumed with his career and being with him so little was difficult for Dixie. His career was taking him in a direction that Dixie didn't want to follow.

Elvis didn't want their relationship to end, but that's the way it had to be. He never told Dixie that he had been unfaithful, but he knew that she knew, and he knew that she forgave him. He also knew it wasn't a life for a decent Christian girl. He too thought it might not be the life for any sort of Christian, but he thought he could handle it; if he couldn't he would simply return to Memphis.

It was Dixie who told Elvis's mama their relationship was over, and they cried. They agreed they would always remain friends because they had a common bond....Elvis.

Dixie's mama asked her what she would do if she married someone else, and then Elvis returned, and told her he made a mistake; that he didn't want that kind of life....that he wanted her to be his wife. Dixie told her she would simply get a divorce, and live with Elvis. It sounded simple enough, but it sure wouldn't have been. She could have very young children by then, and if her hubby was a great guy and a loving father and husband would she really have a desire to get a divorce? Would her love for Elvis remain strong enough to actually do this? It doesn't matter because it didn't happen.

The last time she visited with Elvis was when his mother died. It was a very sad time for them, and probably still remains some of Elvis/Jesse's saddest moments.

Dixie retired from a thirty year career as Pastor's Administrator Assistant. She remained married. In fact she was married for fifty plus years, and raised a beautiful family.
When she was encouraged to write a book about her relationship with Elvis she always refused; she even refused interviews. She didn't want to cheapen the memory of her first love. And she didn't want their relationship to be the event that defined her. More than that, she didn't want to open her private life to public scrutiny. She finally agreed to an interview with Peter in 1990, and it took place in the basement of her church....the same church where she first saw Elvis. Peter says it was one of the most emotional interviews he has ever done....it was clear it was an emotional investment for Dixie as well.

'*Elvis in the Twilight of Memory*,' written by June Juanico, was published in 1997, by Arcade Publishing Inc. It is a tender love story that is sure to give you moisture moments. The sadness I felt for the two of them remained with me for several weeks. June touched my heart and I am sure she will touch yours as will. This is a book you will not want to put aside until you have reached the end.

June's girlfriend invited her to see Elvis perform in their home town; Biloxi, Mississippi. Her girlfriend was excited over the possibility of meeting Elvis. June wasn't the least bit interested. She had been dating a young man for six months and thought he was the most gorgeous man she had ever seen. And then Elvis spotted her June 20, 1955. She was seventeen, and he was twenty. Elvis was smitten, and asked her to show him the town.

From the beginning they were together for hours every day. There romance truly began as a summer romance.

Early in their relationship Elvis was possessive and often showed signs of jealousy. He soon wanted her at his beck and call. She promised not to date any other guys as long as he refrained from dating. He wanted to marry her, and told her he wanted her to be the mother of his children. However, he said he had to wait at least three years. The colonel had control of his personal life, and he believed marriage would ruin his career. In any case, they were young and had plenty of time. Elvis looked forward to the time he would be allowed to make such decisions for himself.

June gave Elvis the book, 'The Prophet, written by Kahlil Gibran. It remained one of his favorite books. It is well known that Elvis has a love for books, and is a deep thinker. I wonder if the gift of this book sparked his love for learning.

As Elvis's career blossomed it was difficult for his mama to share him with the world. However, she never found it difficult to share him with his girlfriends. Gladys wanted Elvis to have a home and a family. She dreamed of having grandchildren. Basically she wanted Elvis to be happy. It troubled her to see his life change so rapidly. She loved him more than life itself. I can identify with that feeling. Elvis was a devoted son; his mama could possibly have been his greatest love.

When Elvis and June introduced their parents to each other there was an immediate bond. Gladys and June loved each other from the start and spent lots of time together when Elvis was not in Memphis.

A juvenile court judge in Jacksonville, Florida said his bumps and grinds were objectionable for teenagers. He ordered Elvis to tone down his act, and informed him that a warrant had already been issued for his arrest if he made any wrong moves. There were policemen in the audience prepared to issue the warrant. Gads! In my opinion it was ridiculous and totally absurd.

June enjoyed touring, but she wished Elvis's life was different. She was eighteen when he recorded, 'Love Me Tender.' At first he called her every day. He missed her and he told her he loved her more than she could know. He thought it would be a sin to waste a love like theirs. After awhile he called her every three or four days. June said Elvis was insecure, but I imagine she began feeling a bit insecure. Many times Elvis would assure her that he would always be hers and hers alone.

Three weeks passed and June had not heard from him. She learned from his mama that he was in Vegas, and didn't know when he would be home. Then she read in the paper that he was at home in Memphis, and had a Vegas showgirl visiting him. He didn't call Christmas, and by then June read he had a different Vegas showgirl in Memphis.

Finally, a couple of days after Christmas he called. He told her he had tried to call on Christmas day, but couldn't get through. He made no mention of their long separation and lack of phone calls. He casually asked if she had a good Christmas. After hearing her response he asked if anything was wrong. Gads! I swear....will not literally, but it seemed like there was two Elvis Presley's in his mind. After a short conversation he wished her a Happy New Year....in case he didn't have an opportunity to call her on New Year's Day.

June didn't mind sharing him with fans, but she would not accept his involvement with other women. She decided to forget him because she was sure he would never have a life of his own.

She went on a date....a real date; an early movie, dinner, and dancing; I was stunned. She was tired of staying home while Elvis womanized, so she accepted a date with a very handsome man, who was ten years older. He had been married only two years before divorcing. June said they had so much fun that neither of them wanted the date to end. She knew Elvis would never be able to date her so openly. They had a whirlwind romance, and within a few weeks they fell in love. She quickly accepted his marriage proposal. Elvis had not called her in all that time; however, I think she was a bit hasty.

Mid-March 1957, Elvis finally sent her a telegram. He wanted her to meet him in New Orleans. She had mixed emotions about making this trip. She wondered how she would feel when they were finally together again. She had to tell him the truth, and feel no regrets. When she saw him her heart skipped a beat as he ran to meet her. He scooped her up into his arms and gave her a quick kiss. Then he put her down, took hold of her hand, and they ran to a train that was waiting for them. After they got inside he pulled her up into his arms. He carried her to his private car, and immediately began kissing her. He told her he had missed her, and he thought she just might not make the trip. Then he held her at arm's length, and told her she looked wonderful. He had not given her a chance to say anything. Perhaps she was surprised at his behavior, and simply didn't know what to say. And perhaps she didn't know what she wanted to say.

Elvis was so excited to see her that he couldn't stop talking before he said, "I'm not letting you out of my sight. You're coming home with me baby. Wait till you see the surprise I have for you. You're gonna s _ _ _ when you see what I bought for you."

June fought her feelings, and then blurted out that she couldn't go home with him… because she didn't have any clothes. He told her they could shop for a whole new wardrobe when they got home. She then told him she didn't make plans to go home with him. Still excited he said, "The only plans you need are to spend your life with me." He had already told his mama June was coming home with him. Elvis was going to settle down with a southern girl who simply wanted to be a wife and mother. Elvis's mama thought June was perfect for Elvis. Elvis told June as soon as they arrived in Memphis they would call her mama.

June never traveled alone. She usually invited her girlfriend, Pat, to travel with her. Pat was waiting in another car for June to return. June told Elvis they were in Pat's dad's car and that Pat couldn't drive back to Biloxi by herself. Gad's! She certainly was having a difficult time telling him she was engaged. Elvis quickly told her he would have one of the guys drive Pat back. He was so anxious for her to see her surprise; he knew she was going to love it.

June said Elvis kissed her after almost every word. She clearly was avoiding telling him why she made the trip to see him. Throughout his excitement she kept thinking about Fabian. She said Fabian needed her....Elvis didn't. She didn't want to break Fabian's heart, and besides they were in love. She was convinced she would never be able to trust Elvis with her heart; he would never be faithful to her. Even if he intended to be... it simply wouldn't happen with all his temptations and desires. She had to quit stalling. While I was reading I wondered why the train hadn't left the station since they had arrived late.

Finally, she blurted out, "I can't go home with you Elvis...I'm engaged to be married." Elvis slumped down on the couch, and put his head in his hands. When he looked up at her his expression was one of disbelief. June fought to hold her tears, but I couldn't hold mine. It was truly a moisture moment for me. When my eyes began to leak there was no stopping the flow. I felt their hurt, and I felt his disbelief. He was hoping she wasn't serious. He was hoping she was just trying to get even with him for his neglect. When she told him she was serious he lowered his head in his hands again.

The train gave a jerk as the conductor yelled, "All aboard." June leaned to kiss Elvis on the forehead, and then she said, "I love you Elvis Presley....I always will. Take care of yourself." Then she ran from the car, grabbed Pat's hand, and they jumped from the train; then her tears flowed. She looked back at the moving train, and saw Elvis leaning out the door; he was waving. Joyce waved and blew him a kiss.

A headline in the next day's newspaper read, 'Elvis buys Graceland.' June wondered if that was the big surprise that she was going to love.

Ten weeks later June and Fabian were married. Twenty-four days after they were married June's mama called her. She waited until Fabian had gone to work. She told June... 'Elvis called and wants you to meet him the next afternoon at four o'clock at Union Station in New Orleans.' And then he asked how June was. He sounded surprised to learn that June actually was married.

June didn't go, but Pat and some of her friends did. When they arrived they learned Elvis had gotten off the train in Lafayette, Indiana. He drove to Memphis alone in a rented car.

A few weeks later June began to cry when she and Pat were talking about Elvis. Pat told her she should have believed that Elvis truly loved her instead of being afraid he would break her heart. Then she asked June if she ever thought about his heart. June vowed to make her marriage perfect....It was the only way for her to survive.

Six years' after June was married she participated in a bowling tournament in Memphis. Elvis was now one of the most famous people in the world. She hoped to see him, but she thought he was still making movies in Hollywood.

June introduced herself to the guard at the Graceland gate. He told her Elvis wasn't home, but that he was at the theatre in town. So June and her teammates went to the theatre. June was ushered to Elvis and his date. She walked behind him, and tapped him on the shoulder. Elvis was excited and surprised to see her. After a nice conversation he invited her and the team to visit Graceland the following night. They hugged and kissed.

When they arrived at Graceland the guard told them Elvis had sent regrets. He would not be able to see them because he was having personal problems. They were disappointed. June wondered if he was really dealing with personal problems, or did he have second thoughts about seeing her. At that time newspapers and magazines were talking about his current love affair with Ann Margaret and his live-in girlfriend, Priscilla.

The 1969, Hurricane Camille, did lots of damage to Biloxi. Fabian sent June and the children to Vegas to stay with his brother while he stayed in Biloxi to help where he was needed. His brother was a casino boss where Elvis was headlining. They went to a show, and went home directly afterwards. Upon their arrival her brother-in-law called backstage of the International, and said, "June wants to talk to Elvis." The phone was handed to Elvis, and they had a heart to heart talk.

June told him she was worried about him because he appeared to be hyper on stage. He told her not to worry about him. He told her when he needed to 'unwind' he read his favorite book, 'The prophet'....the book June gave him. He had read it many times. June told him to take care of himself and said, "I love you."

Elvis responded, "I love you too June....Take care baby."

'My Love Affair with Elvis: Don't Ask Forever,' written by Joyce Bova, as told to William Conrad Nowels, was published in 1995, by Kensington Publishing Corporation. Joyce had nearly a two year love affair with Elvis. She used her diaries to write her story. She was a junior staff member of the Armed Services Committee of the United States House of Representatives Investigative Subcommittee. When she met Elvis she was very discreet about their relationship. Her identical twin sister, Janice, was the only person who knew the details from the very beginning. Sometime later close friends on and off the hill were told.

They met the summer of 1969. She and a friend, who also worked on the hill, decided they needed a vacation to escape some of the frenzy at work. August 16, 1969 they boarded a TWA flight. Three days later they would meet Paul Anka and Elvis. The hotel arranged ringside seats to see Paul. He noticed them while he performed, and after the show he invited them backstage. He told Joyce he would like to take her out for dinner the following night, and her friend was invited too. She declined his invitation because they intended to see Elvis's show. Paul told them unless they had VIP reservations they would not get tickets. However, he could guarantee they would get in. He told them to pick up their tickets at the VIP line, and meet him in the lobby after the show.

While they were waiting in line they were approached by a staff person who asked if they would like to meet Elvis right then between shows. They were amazed at their good fortune. They entered a room full of other hopefuls wanting to see him. Elvis noticed Joyce, and took an immediate interest in her. From that first moment he used endearing language when talking to her; she was hooked. When he learned she had not yet seen his show he told one of the guys to seat the girls in his booth. He wanted to see Joyce after the show. Her memory of that night is written from the heart. She leaves the reader with a feeling of excitement and, a strong desire to continue reading. She is brilliant in her word usage, and she delivers an extremely explicit description of their relationship. I was actually a bit uncomfortable at times. She shares so many details that I thought I was intruding in Elvis's very private.... personal life.

I've learned Elvis is a 'toucher.' I too am a 'toucher.' From the moment he is attracted to someone he is touchy/feely. He wants to keep his gals close to him, by his side, holding hands, or arms around them. He reels them in.

Joyce was enjoying watching Elvis relate to the many ticket holders who wanted to meet him that she forgot she and Ann Marie were supposed to meet Paul in the lobby. She didn't want to leave, so Ann Marie went by herself. Joyce had a strict Catholic upbringing, so when Elvis invited her to his suite for dinner she didn't show an immediate interest. She told him she didn't want to be his girl of the night. He quickly made it clear that he knew she was a nice girl, and he would be a perfect gentleman. He told her she ought to realize it is physically impossible for him to be with a girl every night, and do what he does on stage. When she mentioned the fact he was married he told her he just wanted someone to talk to. He was intrigued when he learned Joyce is an identical twin. She was twenty-four. She thought she could differentiate between reality and fantasy, and now she was in a situation that threatened to obliterate the thin line between them. She had already been mistaken for Priscilla when she was in his private booth, and it made her very nauseous. Joyce barely touched her food. I chuckled when I read that she felt foolish because she expected a nice quiet dinner, and it turned out to be munching on a hamburger with the guys. She would soon learn their relationship, most times, would include the guys. The guys welcomed her into the group.

Elvis was intrigued with Joyce's job on the hill. Government was very interesting to him and he was faithful in supporting our country in any way he could.

From their very first meeting she felt that even if he had not been the fabulous Elvis Presley, the king of Rock and Roll; his effect on her would be absolutely the same. Before he requested she be taken down to a cab he told her he wanted to see her again. He told her he would call her; and he did. From the very beginning they had a relaxed connection. He arranged for the girls to set in his booth once again, and invited them to dinner; cheeseburgers served on expensive china. Elvis told her he was just a man. He was not 'the King'... or any of the stuff that was published about him.

When it was time for her to return to DC Elvis wanted more time with her. He wanted them to get to know each other. She told him she wanted to stay, but the Congress of the United States did not recess for her. After kissing her again and again he asked for her phone number. She quickly wrote it on a piece of paper, folded it, and handed it to him. He placed a small ring in her palm. She describes it as being an exquisite diamond set in beautifully wrought gold. He said he wasn't going to give her a chance to forget him....as if she could or would.

Joyce describes herself as being a woman of extreme intense emotions. If she gives herself she gives herself heart and soul. Her feelings are too focused to be spread around. And now she was focused on Elvis.

Their relationship was kept secret because she did not want to go public because of her position on the hill. She didn't want their relationship turned into a 'messy situation.' It was enough that she was an adulterous; the other woman, and she didn't want to create any problems for Elvis. He wasn't concerned for himself, but he didn't want Joyce hurt, so he respected her decision.

A week later he called her at two in the morning. He was in California. He asked if she were still running the government. He missed her, and wanted her to make a trip to see him. Janice was just getting home. Elvis wanted to talk to her, and to prove that he was Elvis he sang a bit of, 'She's not you.' Later, Joyce questioned whether she wanted to open herself to the kind of hurt and rejection that seemed inevitable in trying to have a romance with him. She wondered if the chemistry they had was strong enough for something to really come of it. She was confident that he sensed from the beginning that she just plain liked him as a person. When he picked up on this he didn't let his stardom get between them. He was genuine and down to earth. She would soon learn that he had a fragile human being living inside him. And she was falling in love despite her sister's concerns, despite all common sense and logic, and despite her own misgivings.

Elvis had a difficult time taking 'no' for an answer. He often was excited when he called her, and told her she was going to do something; instead of asking. One day he told her not to play 'too' hard to get. She tried to assure him that she wasn't, and then she asked him to remember that she worked for the Congress of the United States. Her job was very important to her. She had worked hard to accomplish all that she had and she enjoyed her work. She didn't want to lose her job; even for Elvis Presley. But at the same time she wanted to do all the things he wanted her to.

She was concerned about his marriage. He had told her more than once that his marriage was ending soon. It was the only way she could envision giving herself to him, heart, body, and soul. She was confident that making a commitment to him was not like making a commitment to any other man. It was important to her to remain strong an independent.

When he returned to Las Vegas Joyce invited one of her closest friends, on the hill, to make the trip with her. After the show she told Elvis he was spectacular, but noticed he didn't do the somersaults. It was now just too much for him. She reminded him the Gatorade he drank was full of chemicals, and not good for him. He laughed and told her he worked too hard keeping his body in shape to ever put anything harmful in it. Oh! How I wish that were so. I believe he meant it, but it would not be long before it was clear he lacked simple common sense....at least in this regard he did. I've often wondered how very intelligent minds could lack common sense.

Elvis was glad they didn't arrive two days earlier. Someone called the hotel to report he was going to be kidnapped. Then a member of the Memphis Mafia received a call that Elvis was going to be 'blown away.' Then the hotel received a souvenir menu that had a picture of Elvis printed on it with a drawing of a gun pointing to his head. The FBI was notified. Elvis was advised to cancel his shows; he refused. As he was talking he appeared to have lots of nervous energy; he couldn't or didn't stop moving. His face was scratched from girls clawing and grabbing at him. He commented that he wanted to yank them out of their seats and throw them up into the balcony. He loved the fans, but enough is enough.

It's amazing how a second can change life so drastically. The dialogue between them was astonishing. Elvis showed a side she had not fully grasped before. Joyce walked out on him and returned to home. Janice reminded her that she got along without him for twenty-four years, and she could get along without him another twenty-four. Joyce wasn't so sure she wanted to. She had just arrived home, and she missed him already.

Months passed before she received a phone call at work from a friend of Elvis's. He told her Elvis was in Washington, and wanted to see her. Elvis apologized for the way he behaved in Vegas. She didn't want to open herself up to more heartache, but the moment she heard his voice all the excitement, passion, and joy returned. Life was worth living again. Joyce believed in second chances.

They talked about how they met and why he was attracted to her. He opened up about his feelings for Priscilla. He thought Joyce deserved an explanation. He had known Priscilla since she was a little girl. He taught her how to dress, how to act; basically everything. They spent very little time together, and just drifted apart. The marriage was about over, otherwise he wouldn't have made the trip to see her.

I don't know if he actually made the trip to see President Nixon and then decided to contact Joyce, or the other way around. Course he told Joyce he was on the plane before he thought of meeting the President. Elvis did accomplish a 'mission impossible.' Joyce knew it was quite difficult to get 'any' appointment with the President of the United States, and getting one immediately was virtually impossible. He then showed her the badge President Nixon gave him; it was official. He was an agent at large for the Bureau of Narcotics and Dangerous Drugs. Elvis wanted so much to tell our youth about the danger of drugs.

This was the first of many days she would call her work to report she was ill. It is amazing she didn't lose her job; she came close, but they really liked her so gave her a lot of rope, and hoped she wouldn't hang herself, and she didn't.

Sonny West was with him and he placed the order for room service; Jon Burrows, suite 506. I grinned from ear to ear because that is the name he used when we met. He spoke of the disadvantages fame and adulation can bring. He couldn't go to a movie or walk in the park. It hadn't occurred to me he had never been inside a bank. He said most of the time he feels like an animal, on display, in a zoo. How sad is that? Who knew?

He wanted to immediately get through to Joyce when he called, so she had an 'Elvis' phone installed.

Sonny accompanied Elvis to DC December 30, 1970. Joyce's workload was heavy, but she chose to be late so she could meet Elvis at eight. He told Joyce he loved her, so she told him she would never take his ring off until one of them no longer loved the other.

Elvis gave her a pill that would help her relax, so she would awake from her sleep bright eyed. This was one of those times when I wanted to clobber the both of them. It was very difficult for me to wrap my brain around this 'stupidity.' I was very disappointed in them, and without reading another word; I could see the writing on the wall. She said it took effect with unbelievable swiftness. However, within minutes she was not asleep or even sleepy. Instead, she experienced a sensation unlike any she had felt before. Her body felt weightless as if she were suspended in space. At times it seemed her body was spinning in mid-air. At the same time she knew she was lying on the bed like a corpse. She was unable to move a muscle; her eyelids were frozen in place. A while later they had a mumbled conversation. It was frightening. Joyce said her words came out in a voice that didn't belong to her. However, she felt absolutely invigorated when she woke.

She had already missed another day at work and couldn't possibly miss two consecutive days. Once again he told her to take a pill to help her sleep. She declined. He had talked to doctors, and he was as knowledgeable as they were about prescription drugs. Without another word she swallowed the pill. Then she asked herself, 'What harm can such a tiny pill do?' For Pete's sake, it seems to me she got a good lesson the night before. If you're taking a pill to put you to sleep did she really believe her reaction to the first pill worked the way it should have to achieve a normal sleep? Once again when she woke she felt livelier than she had in days. Wasn't that another clue linked to the tiny pill?

Their relationship was full of him calling to tell her she was going to meet him when and where; and her feeling bad because she desperately wanted to, but couldn't get the time off at work. So it always ended with Joyce telling him she couldn't leave her job every time he wanted her to.

One night she was brooding over how she could be with him as much as he demanded, and still fulfill her responsibilities on the hill. Then the 'Elvis phone' rang. As she walked to it she wished she knew how to be an independent woman as well as a cherished and loved one as well. She needed both. "Joyce, I open Vegas next week and I want you out there with me when I do." She so wanted to and she didn't want to continue telling him she was needed on the hill; but she was. "You just tell me who to talk to. I'll take care of it. I'll get you the time off.

I don't remember what was going on at work, but it was important for her to be there. The chairman had already made it quite clear that he would not look kindly on anyone calling in sick. I chuckled during the rest of the conversation. Elvis told her he would talk to Nixon. Joyce thought, 'Ye Gads! Joyce and I were on the same wave length. I'm chuckling as I write this. It seems so absurd to me, but to Elvis it was a natural thing to do. I immediately thought of him saying, 'I'm just a man who has a famous brother. I was reminded that even then Elvis was just a man.....a very talented, charismatic man, but still....just a man. Bless his heart.

Joyce told him his power might be limitless in his world, but it wasn't in hers. She told him he couldn't call the President of the United States about her, and reminded him she was not a member of Congress. Elvis was still determined to call him. She pleaded with him not to make the call, and then she promised she would be in Vegas at least for the close if she couldn't make it for the opening. He wasn't happy, but he always accepted the compromise, and anxiously looked forward to them being together.

I think if he had asked the President to work things out, so Joyce could have the time off, the President would have thought he was smoking pot.

Elvis returned to Graceland when he closed in Vegas. Not long after, Joyce received a call at work; Elvis wanted her with him. Once again she told him she couldn't take time off. One of the guys told her not to be alarmed, but Elvis was in the hospital. He wouldn't tell her what was wrong over the phone. She hurriedly said she would call back with her arrival time. When she arrived she was told they had to hurry. Elvis had been released and was waiting in a private plane on the tarmac. Joyce was nearly being dragged. "We gotta hurry. We're going to Graceland."

His diagnosis was secondary glaucoma and inflamed eyes. When they arrived at Graceland the doctor was waiting. The doctor gave Joyce a vial of pills with instructions to give them to Elvis during the night. About two in the morning he was taken to another room where medical equipment was set up. Elvis requested that Joyce remain at his side. He became more alert as the examination continued. The doctor gave him an injection....directly into the eyeball.... after he said, "No anesthesia is possible here." Joyce said her blood ran cold. I nearly fainted when I read about it. Elvis sat up straight and braced himself. Joyce squeezed his hand as tight as she could. The doctor moved in close with the needle. Elvis didn't move. The doctor removed the needle, and sighed with relief. I imagine they all did. He was helped back to his bed. He slept until the next afternoon except for the times Joyce woke him for his medication. He grew stronger every day, and Joyce was happy she could be with him when he needed her.

When he wasn't sleeping he talked about the books he read and studied. Joyce had not taken a sleep aid since she arrived at Graceland. However, the night before she returned home she took one and asked if he would give her a few to take back with her; he gave her a full vial. Once again, I could see the writing on the wall.

A few days after she arrived home the news reported Elvis's eye infection. There was just one little incorrect detail. Priscilla was the loyal and concerned wife who was by his side through the crisis; she nursed him back to health.

Several days later the 'Elvis phone' rang early in the morning. The moment she arrived at Graceland she was sent upstairs. Elvis once again told her he wanted her with him all the time. He wanted her to move into Graceland. She didn't need to work; he would take care of her. She was determined not to lose her independence; not even for Elvis.

She met Elvis's Uncle Vester and 'Dodger,' his grandmother. Dodger told her not to wait too long to have children because a woman should have plenty. From the moment Elvis met Joyce it appeared he was attracted to her personality as well as her looks. They had a great rapport. The ten years age difference was not an issue.

When Elvis was ready to work on a new album he wanted her 'good ear and honest opinion.' She said Elvis could sing a Mickey Mouse song, and it would be a classic. Elvis never shut her out, and she was happy that he made her a part of his world. Once he opened the door and invited her in he didn't close it.

Several times Elvis showed signs of jealousy. This was a behavior started with his first girlfriend, and he never seemed to be able to control it. He was positive that she was pursued by the politicians on the hill. She tried to assure him no one on the hill showed any interest in her, and she had no interest in any of them.

One of the books he kept on his nightstand was, 'The Physicians' Desk Reference.' He had told her if doctors' learned about drugs by reading it then he could too.

Joyce over-slept and missed her plane. But, it was Saturday so she rescheduled for Sunday. That night they had a lengthy conversation. I don't remember what happened to cause them to discuss politics, but I do remember something they heard on television sparked it. I was touched by what Joyce said, because I feel the exact same way. "I think what makes this the greatest country in the world is that you can boo the President and burn the flag. And that no secret police come at four in the morning, and drag you away. Maybe what the flag really stands for is the freedom to burn it, and to not lose your right to life, liberty, and the pursuit of happiness." I hope reading this gives you warm, fuzzy feelings, and that you might even get 'goose bumps.'

Joyce beat herself up for asking for the prescription of the sleep aid. It scared her, and she finally became worried about her level of dependency. She prayed for the strength to talk to Elvis about his use. She thought this was the most important thing she could ever do for them; for them both. She knew she had delayed this conversation long enough

She was needed at Graceland. She couldn't say 'no' to him. He simply missed her. She wasn't the least bit angry that he considered her work unimportant compared to his need to be with her. The mood had been set. She expected a warm, cozy, romantic evening. Once again it didn't happen....however, 'something' happened, and it left a lot to be desired.

On her flight home she worried about facing Janice. She thought of what Janice always told her when she left; 'Be careful.' She arrived too late to go to work. Her life began caving in on her. She was extremely depressed. All she wanted to do was take the sleep aid and go to bed.

The following morning her supervisor called for her to meet him in his office. She was fortunate he didn't fire her, but he did give her a stern warning. He told her he knew she couldn't have been ill all the Fridays and Mondays that she missed work; and it had to stop immediately.

Weeks passed before the 'Elvis phone' rang. He had been busy. He was back in Vegas, and wanted her with him. This was finally a good time for her because Congress would be in recess, but she didn't know if she could face him. She didn't know what to do; she was pregnant.

It was difficult finding the right time to tell him about the baby. She just didn't find an opening. He fell asleep, his entourage showed up early, or whatever. She knew it had to be done before she left him the next time.

Elvis wanted to buy her a new car; one that was heavy enough for her not to worry about having serious injuries' in an accident. She thought this was the opening she was looking for.

She asked why he didn't talk about his baby. Lisa Marie was three years old. He said she was a great little girl, and that he spoiled her. I remember seeing Lisa wearing a fur coat when she was very young. Joyce asked about her mother. He told her that once a woman becomes a mother she changes. She asked what he meant. He told her when a woman has a child its God's way of telling her she is no longer a child. He doesn't think a mama should be sexy or make herself attractive to men. Gads! Where did that come from? I was about knocked off my chair. In his way of thinking it simply wasn't right. He told her a woman was no longer attractive, 'in that way,' after she becomes a mama. Joyce was devastated. She told him that not every woman would lose her appeal just because she had a baby. But he was adamant and told her it was not exciting, and it's not supposed to be. Then he told her to 'trust him' on this. He was convinced he was right. He drifted off to sleep. Joyce vowed not to tell him she was pregnant, and she cried herself to sleep.

She thought about her options. She couldn't have a baby and Elvis's love. It seemed cruel that the one thing their love created would cause them to have a life separated from each other. She could have the baby, and raise it alone, or she could have an abortion. She never considered adoption. She loved Elvis, and didn't want their relationship to end; she chose abortion. My heart ached when I read what she had done. When it was over she went home and took a sleep aid.

The 'Elvis phone' rang. She could barely talk to him. She was angry and deep into self-pity. I imagine that would be normal behavior under the circumstance. He could tell something was wrong, so she told him she had work problems. He wanted her to tell him about it, so he could make some calls. And after he closed in Vegas he would make a trip to see her. She wasn't ready to see him, so she told him there was nothing he could do.

It took her a long time to talk about the abortion. She couldn't face the truth that she didn't have enough faith in herself to bring a life into the world and raise it alone. And the thought that she chose a relationship with Elvis instead of motherhood troubled her. I imagine she didn't really face it for twenty-three years; when she wrote her book.

A week later the 'Elvis phone' rang and it rang every few days. She was not ready to see him so she let it ring. She didn't reply to the messages left at her work either. She was feeling better physically, but she had a long way to go emotionally. One day she answered; by now she wanted to hear his voice. (I would have put on a CD) It was, Charlie Hodge, one of the guys; telling her Elvis was worried about her. She lied and said she had been taking care of her mother.

She had a difficult time dealing with her emotions. She hadn't found a way to release her anger. She continued to ask herself, why was Elvis's behavior so troublesome. How could he have such warped thinking? She was trying to forgive him for something he wasn't even aware he had done.

They had been apart three months. She worried that he would somehow know she had aborted his baby. But when they saw each other all the loving feelings returned; she was no longer angry.

He again told her he wanted to buy her a new car. She was concerned what the people on the hill would think when they learned about it, so she declined. When he wanted to know her favorite color she told him she didn't have one. He laughed and told her everyone has a favorite color. He then asked her to pick one. Since Halloween had just passed she blurted out, "orange." He laughed again, and told her orange wasn't anyone's favorite color and the conversation was changed to another subject.

Elvis surprised her with a new orange Pinto. He reminded her that it was just what she wanted; orange and little. She was excited; she loved it. He told her if her favorite color was red, black, or white she would have saved them a lot of time. It was the only orange car in the area.

Joyce learned touring was a lot different than a Vegas show. Elvis was in his element, and he excitedly explained his feelings. He felt close to the people who came to see him on tour. He didn't want to disappoint them. He knew many of them had saved a long time for this moment. He realized a lot of those in the crowd would never be able to see him in Vegas even if they could get in the auditorium. He told her these are the people who got him where he is, and he wanted them to know he was grateful for their interest, loyalty, and love.

She was disappointed he didn't sing, 'The First Time Ever I Saw Your Face.' He apologized, and told her it wasn't the kind of song that would work with the show. She told him she understood, and quickly changed the subject. She looked forward to the show in Baltimore because her family and friends would be there.

Once Elvis began learning he didn't stop. I believe he is a much better person for it because he followed his heart. In the event that you don't know, Elvis is extremely intelligent, and spent lots of time reading books that would challenge his mind. I imagine he has had an extra ordinary and remarkable journey. And at the time of this writing it is not over yet. He told Joyce he needed someone with him who could understand the things he is about....Someone he can talk to about the knowledge he is absorbing. He had a desire....a need to reach people. The Lord had given him the platform to awaken the minds of millions of people. He wondered if that was his destiny….his reason for birth. He believed it very well may be. He was confident he had discovered the master plan. He had a terrific need….a desire to pay back his fans for everything they had given him. He could do this by sharing his knowledge.

In 1971 on the flight to Louisville Elvis told Joyce that if he had to he could easily go back to poverty. In fact, he had even thought of doing just that. Now remember he dreamed of returning to the simple life for years. And don't we know that dreams really do come true? We simply have to pray about it, be patient, and know it is all in the Lords time.

The following morning she groped her way into the bathroom. She didn't like the face staring back at her. She felt a serpent had reared its ugly head. Her tongue was thick, her stomach ached, and her mouth was dry.

She knew Elvis had guys protecting him, helping him, etc, but it concerned her to learn they were all, 'yes men.' They loved him, but not enough to protect him from himself. It was clear he was his own worst enemy. She was worried that his dependence on his prescriptions would kill him. I imagine she wondered how he could be so intelligent, and yet so stupid at the same time. She often wondered if it was up to her to prevent him from destroying himself. She had tried, but had she tried enough?

One of the sweetest things I have ever heard of happened in Baltimore. Joyce's family and friends were in the audience of twenty thousand who were showing Elvis an extreme welcome. After he sang the first few numbers he stepped to center stage, and gestured the crowd to be quiet. He stood still and waited for the stomping, whistling and screaming to stop. When it was totally quiet he looked in Joyce's direction. Then he said, into the microphone, "Joyce, this is for you." The music began, but he yelled to the band, "Stop, please stop. That's not right. I want this to be perfect;" and it was. The crowd applauded. Joyce's family and friends were buzzing. Until then they didn't have a clue Elvis and Joyce were an item. Joyce's mascara had smeared her face with the help of her tears. This was another moisture moment for me. It was clear Elvis wanted the world to know he loved Joyce. He sang, "The First Time Ever I Saw Your Face." Joyce was radiating happiness. Elvis is definitely a romantic. Perhaps that would have been a good business venture for him after August 16, 1977; schools to teach men how to be romantic. It certainly is well known there is a need for them. Perhaps this will give someone an idea to pursue it.

Elvis surprised Joyce. He told her Priscilla had given them an early Christmas present....his freedom; the divorce would be final soon. They had just a few details to work out. He again told her to think about moving into Graceland. That's exactly what she had dreamed of and wanted, but now she was in shock. It was actually happening. She told him she would have to think about what it would actually mean....how it would change things.

She wanted to call Janice to wish her a happy birthday, and to tell her what had happened. Elvis suggested they fly to DC. They flew on a commercial flight. He signed autographs and visited with the passengers. He was in his element, and he was happy.

However, at the same time he was so unpredictable that she wondered if she could ever truly know him. She was troubled because he got her started using sleep aid with the promise it wouldn't hurt her; but it did. She didn't like that she was now dependent on it.

Just before Christmas Elvis was bursting with desire; it was Joyce who didn't have it. I take that back....she had it, but it was for the sleep aid. He snuggled close, but she turned away. She didn't plan it....she just suddenly didn't respond to him as she always had....as she always wanted too. She thought about her actions, and then realized it wasn't sudden.

It had happened gradually. She couldn't explain her change of heart....She didn't understand it.

A month later, she returned to Graceland for Elvis's thirty-seventh birthday. She gave him a ring. It was a simple gold band with 'love' inscribed on it. A tiny diamond was inside the 'O,' and Elvis loved it.

That night they took their sleep aid, and Elvis began reading aloud. He had given Joyce a few books, but she hadn't read them yet. He was anxious for her to read them, so they could discuss them. She was to leave the next morning, but there was a storm warning. Janice convinced her to listen to Elvis, and not leave until morning. That night was a repeat of the night before. As he read aloud he told her one phase of his life was ending. He told her he was celebrating his thirty-seventh birthday, and he was thinking about his fortieth. He told her forty would be too late. She asked him, "Too late for what?" He told her there was a lot to talk about, and he wanted her answer soon. He then told her he was past the age Jesus was crucified, and he couldn't wait too much longer to plan the rest of his life's work. He told her a phase had definitely ended. She asked him to explain, but he simply responded that someday she would understand.

When she went to his next show she was amazed that for the first time his performance left no impression on her. She couldn't shake the pill incident from her mind. She sat through the festivities after the show with no pleasant emotions.

This night Elvis was in a philosophical mood. He told her he had learned so much from reading and studying. He was searching and finding, He explained that we all have divinity inside us. He related that silence is sacred, and is the resting place of the soul. It's necessary for new thoughts to be born.

She suggested his vision was altered, or induced by the pills, and reminded him of all the side effects being discovered;

and so she worries about it, and about him. He replied that pretty women shouldn't worry, and that he hired people to do the worrying. She couldn't believe they were actually having an intelligent discussion. She was amazed that he remained composed, and showed no sign of anger.

She shared the feelings in her heart. Part of her wanted to be with him, and help him in his search for what he was looking for, but another part of her wanted to escape because she was frightened. She knew he was frightened too, but there was a difference. She was frightened because they had a drug dependency, and whatever he was frightened of causes him to take the drugs. She had insight. She had become wise. Maybe now she would help herself even if she couldn't help him.

She told him that he was the man she loved more than she thought she could ever love anyone, and now her heart was breaking. He didn't respond. He was asleep. He was still asleep when she woke the next afternoon. When she was packed and ready to leave she knew what she must do. She removed the ring he gave her when she had promised him she would wear it until they no longer loved each other. She thought, 'I still love you Elvis, but I love you too much to watch you kill yourself.' She placed the ring on the nightstand and leaned over and kissed his cheek. She held back her tears until the elevator doors closed behind her.

I'm happy they had finally shared their thoughts without the anger and resentment. As I read I agreed with much of what he said, so it was easy to understand where he was coming from, but I know you can accomplish this journey without drugs.

Joyce knew their love affair had to end. In spite of her hurt, and the emptiness she felt inside she knows she did the right thing by leaving. She gained back her freedom and a future.

After watching the satellite special from Hawaii she called Charlie Hodge. She had to tell someone how much it meant to her. Sometime later the 'Elvis phone' rang. I imagine it must have been difficult for her to have it disconnected. And

I wonder how long it took her to finally do so. She hesitated for a moment. She didn't want to crumble and begin all over again. However, he was just sweet. He wanted to know how she was, and when she was going to see his show. He missed her. He wanted her to meet him in Los Angeles. He asked for a copy of the photo that was taken of the two of them in the Vegas suite, and he asked if she would call him in two weeks. Without thinking she told him she would....and for a fleeting second I imagine she meant it.

She sent the photo, but she didn't call. She didn't speak to him again either. However, she did see him one more time; a little over two years later in Vegas. The crowd was still screaming and cheering. She didn't stay for the whole show. She wiped her tears from her cheek as she walked out of the hotel. And I set here with my eyes leaking again. I think I need to take a pill....perhaps Celexa.

Two years later, after thinking and talking about it for years, Elvis finally walked into a different lifestyle....He is now just a man.

As I read Joyce's story I had mixed emotions. At times I wanted to shake some sense into her and at times I wanted to give Elvis a 'good talking' too. At times I felt sorry for her. At times I felt sorry for him. And at times I felt sorry for both. Even though it was an interesting read there were times I had to put the book down, and walk away from it for awhile. It was a very emotional story. It amazed me she could write it. I knew she had to re-live the whole experience in order to get it on paper. And it's clear to me that it was one of the most difficult things she had ever done.

There's a song, 'You always hurt the one you love.' It came to mind several times as I read Joyce's story. Elvis was like two personalities. His mood changed quickly. He spoke words of love, and then spoke sarcastically, hateful, or harsh. Often times she noticed his beautiful blue eyes had turned to ice. She was hurt, but she loved him, so she dealt with it. I could not have been as gracious, perhaps because our tempers would have clashed. But anyway, I'm glad I only wanted him to be my younger brother.

'*Elvis and Me*,' written by Priscilla Beaulieu Presley, was published in 1985, by The Berkley Publishing Group. When Elvis met Priscilla she was fourteen, and living in Germany. Elvis, being a southern boy, thought nothing of their age difference or that Priscilla was so young. Marrying young was common in the south....Perhaps it still is. She was an Air force brat, and Elvis had only a few months before he would be discharged from the Army. Priscilla was only in the ninth grade, but he was smitten with her, and it was obvious she returned the feeling. He left Germany the early part of 1960.

Several months passed before he called to ask her to visit him in Los Angeles. Priscilla's parents finally gave their permission, and her father escorted her. After he saw her safely to Elvis he returned to Germany.

Elvis wanted Priscilla to dye her hair black. He wanted her to look like someone he had met years earlier.

It didn't take long for Priscilla to learn Elvis had a temper. He just didn't stop to think or reason. It was a natural thing for him to lose his cool....but from what I've read he was quick to apologize, and that is a good thing.

Elvis introduced Priscilla to sleeping pills. The first time she took them she was out for two days. Gads! She was lucky she woke up.

From the beginning of their relationship Priscilla felt threatened. It was clear she had cause to be jealous; and no doubt insecure. She worked hard at being everything he ever imagined a female could be.

Priscilla didn't want to return to Germany, but her parents were quite adamant that she return as scheduled. After she finished her school year Priscilla gave her parents so much trouble they allowed her to return to Memphis. She was to live with Elvis's dad and new wife, and her young children. And she was to finish school. Priscilla was now sixteen.

Elvis taught her how to dress, how to wear her hair and makeup, how to behave, and even how to walk. I could identify with the walk, because I had been shown how to walk after my dad married the second time; I was about fourteen.

She said Elvis was generous to a fault....with advice. If she did something he didn't like he would correct her. It was extremely difficult to relax under such scrutiny. I can identify with that too.

I was surprised to learn Elvis had a strong aversion for jeans. Apparently they reminded him of his youth; that's all he had to wear. It's strange how values, designs, and styles change. I wonder what Elvis thought when he saw jeans with holes put there intentionally that sold for big bucks...and wealthy people wore them. In fact, poor people couldn't afford to buy them.

Priscilla said Elvis created his own world because, in his environment, he felt comfortable, secure, and protected; comfortable, secure and protected sounds good to me.

In most of the stories I read Elvis was demanding, but he was generous to a fault; he gave often, and to many people. In fact, generally he gave very expensive gifts. He was always aware of and sensitive to everyone's needs.

It is said he got hooked on prescription drugs (speed) in the army. It is also said it is common for soldiers' to take something so they would be assured they would remain awake and alert when they were on night duty....or perhaps any duty. It got out of control because Elvis must have thought more would work faster and better. It usually took him two to three hours to wake up after his bedtime medicine. Many people get hooked using medication thinking the same thing. If it's easy to get hooked on them...it certainly wouldn't be easy to get 'unhooked.' I liken it to weight gain. It's easy to put on, but not easy to take off.

When Priscilla graduated she didn't have a desire to further her education, and Elvis didn't encourage her. Since he is quite intelligent; perhaps a genius, I would think he would want her to continue to learn. He found pleasure in expanding his knowledge through the books he read. I imagine he hoped she would join him in that endeavor.

Priscilla was taking a pill to sleep, a pill to get her going, and she was taking diet pills; she was finally concerned. She didn't like her attitude, or her actions at times. One incident actually frightened her, so she took fewer and fewer pills until she completely stopped. I'm so proud of her for making her own decision, and for being strong enough to follow through with it.

From the beginning of their relationship she had to deal with his involvement with his 'leading ladies.' He told her everything printed about him wasn't true, and that it was all for publicity. I imagine a lot of it was. However, she had already discovered love letters written to him when he was in Germany.

Priscilla soon learned love was far more complicated than she imagined. She wondered how she could continue staying with Elvis when she was positive his future would involve many more temptations; temptations he would not resist.

She got into a real 'tiff' with Elvis over some notes she found; they were very telling. Why he kept them is beyond me. Perhaps it's a man thing. He denied, denied, denied. He accused Priscilla of 'imagining things.' Priscilla was in a cache twenty-two situation. She couldn't challenge him too much because she was afraid he would send her back to her parents. He knew exactly how to keep her under his control. Perhaps he hoped she would find the notes.

Priscilla said that Elvis would lash out due to a simple thing, but it wasn't a simple thing to him. He would yell, and at the same time wink at someone close by. A few minutes later he would be fine while everyone else were bewildered and emotionally depleted.

When Larry Geller became Elvis's barber he also became his spiritual advisor. He introduced Elvis to some great books to help him in his search for a higher spirituality. Priscilla said this is when the relationship changed between them. Elvis told her that if they were to be soul-mates she would also have to join him in his search for the answers to the universe. She tried, but many times she fell asleep shortly after she began reading. Annoyed, Elvis would wake her up, and tell her things would never work out between them because she didn't show interest in him or his philosophies. He reminded her there are a lot of women who would like to read and discuss the books with him. I wonder if he ever found one. Somehow I think he did. Somehow I think he had met her long before he met Priscilla. But due to an unfortunate situation it was not easy for them to be together. But I like to think that after August 16, 1977, what they might have thought was the impossible dream did, in reality, come true.

Elvis lived with Priscilla five years before he proposed marriage. They had talked about having children, but they were not planning on having a child anytime soon. Priscilla looked forward to her time alone with Elvis. However, she knew she would always have to share him with, 'the boys.' Lisa Marie was born exactly nine months after their wedding day, so her time alone with Elvis was cut short.

Priscilla was seven months' pregnant when Elvis told her he thought they should have a trial separation. He said things weren't going right, and he needed time to think. He needed a break. She was numb. Hearing his words must have been devastating.

She instinctively withdrew her affection. She could not forget what he said….how he made her feel, and he definitely left her with a strong sense of doubt.

Priscilla talks about Elvis stomping out the door of Graceland one night, and he didn't return for a few days. He was traveling on his own. Jerry Schilling told her Elvis boarded a commercial airline to Washington DC with the intention of seeing President Nixon. Jerry couldn't very well say Elvis flew from Washington to Los Angeles for him, so he could help find his girlfriend, Joyce, and on their return flight Elvis got the idea to try and see the President. He couldn't very well tell her he called Sonny West from Joyce's apartment to tell him to head for Washington DC because he was needed. Perhaps Priscilla learned about Joyce when her book was published.

For months Elvis and Priscilla were seldom together. They grew apart, but no doubt loved each other if for no other reason than they had a child. Priscilla yearned for more ordinary pleasures. She began to appreciate the simple things she would have liked to share with Elvis, but knew she never could. Elvis was caught off guard. Once again a woman who loved him would leave him.

Priscilla was packed, and ready to leave when she told Elvis he had lost her to a life of her own….not a man, although he was aware of a brief affair, and now there was a 'man in the wings.' They kissed and Priscilla walked to the door.

Priscilla said she placed a bracelet on Elvis's wrist at his funeral. If she did he wasn't in a casket. He would have been standing or sitting beside her. I'm sure Priscilla was in on the events of August 16, 1977 so why on earth would she include some of what she said in her book? I have not included those thoughts here because they are very personal, and did not need to be told. Perhaps she simply doesn't care.

'Are You Lonesome Tonight?' written by Lucy deBarbin and Dary Matera, was published in 1987, by The Berkley Publishing Company. I don't read romance novels, and this is not a novel. However, I believe it's the story of a love that has last a lifetime, and perhaps continues today. After reading this story....I like to think so.

It amazes me that I didn't read this book until recently. I don't know when I purchased it, but I do know it was many years ago; probably sometime in 1988; after I met Elvis. It seems really strange that it would remain packed away or on my bookshelves....unread. It was in this book that I found a yellowed 1988 calendar...just one little piece of paper with Friday, March 12 circled, and the name 'Elvis' printed beside it in pencil. It was a 'special' day. It was the day I met Elvis.

Several have said they were Elvis's one and only true love, and in a couple the author states theirs was his first love. Everyone has an opinion...and I have one too. Lucy is obviously his first; there cannot be two first loves. They met first; they fell in love first. It is as simple as that.

Elvis was eighteen and Lucy sixteen when they met in 1953. He was a young man with a dream of making a career in music. He was unique from the start, but neither of them could possibly know their future. Their first date was exhilarating and it lasted twenty-four years and perhaps beyond. Lucy remained in love with Elvis....not the superstar.

She accepted an invitation to dance at a political party for VIP's somewhere north of Monroe, Louisiana, near the Mississippi border. The party changed the course of her life. Shortly after she arrived she strolled around the property. She noticed a young man wearing a bright blue shirt with big white polka-dots staring at her. It appeared that he wanted to approach her, but was shy.

She hurried back to the house, and told the lady in charge that she needed to leave early, so she was the first to perform. She had never danced in front of a live audience, and the applause and whistles almost blew her away. While she changed clothes she thought she heard Frank Sinatra singing. She peeked out, and saw that it was the young man in the polka-dot shirt. As she rushed out the back door she nearly bumped into the singer. He grabbed her arm to steady her. He smiled, and told her he loved her dance, and she quickly told him she enjoyed his song. She wanted to stay and talk to him, but it was critical that she get home. After quick introductions she had met Elvis Presley. From the beginning she saw something about him that was attractive. He hoped to see her again; she told him she couldn't. She wished him good luck with his singing, and walked through the crowd of people as they complemented her on her dance. When she looked to where Elvis had been standing he was looking at her; their eyes met, they smiled, and she walked away.

I learned something about Elvis I had never heard. Perhaps you don't know this, but in the early days he didn't have his own style. He imitated successful singers such as Frank Sinatra and Dean Martin, or whomever else he chose to copy. And he was very good at it. I'm so glad he decided to be himself.

Two weeks later Lucy agreed to model for a shoot at the Memphis zoo. Mary, the only sister she was close to, lived in Memphis. The photographer and his date invited Mary and Lucy to go with them to the Eagle Nest Club. Lucy was stunned when Elvis appeared on stage. He sang current hits; the songs Dean, Frank, and other popular singers sang. Lucy felt uncomfortable because he looked at her almost the whole time he was singing. She felt a bit flustered because she hadn't quit thinking of him since she met him. After his gig he wandered through the audience being the southern gentlemen that he is and then he stopped at Lucy's table. He asked, "Who's the pretty stranger?" He gave no indication that he remembered her. He was impressed when he learned she was going to model at the zoo. He told her he would like to show her around the beautiful city, but she declined. Mary scolded her for refusing his offer.

After her shoot she had three hours before her ride would arrive, so she went horseback riding. She welcomed the time alone. After about an hour she noticed another rider coming towards her. The horse stopped right beside her. It was Elvis. "Fancy meetin' you again," he said.

She asked, "Why are you following me?" He told her he hadn't stopped thinking of her since they met in Monroe. He just wanted to ride with her a little while. They rode along the edge of the woods. When they came to a place overlooking a lake Elvis got off his horse, and then helped Lucy off hers. They sat on the grass and talked. Lucy asked him about his life, and then Lucy told him a little about herself, and about her love for music. She left out the dark side. She had a secret that she just couldn't share.

When they turned in the horses Elvis asked if he could see her again. She had a difficult time holding back her tears. She had finally met someone kind who treated her like a gentleman should, and she was forced to brush him off. He asked Lucy if she believed in miracles, and then told her he had been with lots of girls, but he saw from the beginning that she had something very special. He began telling her he had read King Arthur and the Knights of the Round Table, and especially liked what he read about Lancelot. Lancelot kept himself pure, and only loved one woman. He told her Lancelot was mixed up, but he could see things that others couldn't. He told Lucy he thought he was like Lancelot. Lucy was impressed with Elvis. He was the kind of man she had always dreamed of and now meeting him seemed cruel. She thought she was better off fantasizing about a prince who didn't exist than being tortured by the knowledge of one who did. He insisted that she go to the club again, and they would go to dinner after. She relented, and told Mary she was going to see Kate Smith who was performing in the city. Mary was so happy that she was going out that she told her to take her car.

While at the club Lucy tried to concentrate on Elvis, but she couldn't get her mind off her problems. After a single set

Elvis told Lucy he was going to show her Memphis. When they drove down a street lined with large, beautiful, colonial homes Elvis told her he was going to live in a house like these one day. He had a plan that required a lot of work, but he was going to make a record. He said a person can get rich if they make a good record, and then asked what she thought. Lucy told him she thought he could do it if he didn't give up. And then she told him that he needed to be different to be noticed.

Elvis stopped near a park and suggested they go for a walk. After a while they sat on a bench, and he asked her to tell him about her life. He wanted to know her dreams, and what she wanted to do with her life. She told him an abridged version of her life....leaving out many things. He told Lucy he would be successful, and buy his mama anything she wanted. Then his face lit up, and he told her he would take care of her mama too if he made it before she did. Excitedly, they embraced. Lucy said it was a loving embrace between kindred spirits, and it felt wonderful. They walked awhile before Elvis leaned to gently kiss her. He asked if he could see her again, and she heard herself saying she guessed so. But how could she. It could only lead to trouble. He noticed her hesitance, and then told her he wanted her to share his success. Lucy smiled, but knew it was quite improbable that she could. They continued to walk awhile before Elvis pointed to the sky, and said, "You see this moon? Remember it. Whenever you see it, think of me, and how we will be together again, soon." She hesitated to give him her phone number, but he persisted until she gave him her work number.

Lucy returned to her bleak routine. Two weeks later Elvis called. He had to see her. She gave him excuses why she couldn't, but he showed up. They went to dinner at a popular, elegant, restaurant in the suburban area. The name of the restaurant was fitting; it was the Rendezvous. Elvis went all out; steaks, etc. Lucy declined the champagne and dessert. Elvis signaled the waiter. Lucy was presented with three fresh red roses with long stems. Pointing to each one he said, "This

one is you. This one is me. And this one represents our love."
Wow! Talk about romantic. Did his mama teach him that or
was it second nature to him? He then told her he wanted to
show her what it means to love someone, and what marriage
is. She was a bit confused by his last comment, but she let
it pass. When they left the restaurant he asked if there was
a pretty place where they could talk. She chose the lake that
weaves through Monroe. Elvis found a secluded spot. They
sat on the bank directly across from the country club. As Elvis
leaned to kiss her his arm got tangled in the gold chain she
wore, and the cross fell into the grass. They couldn't find it,
so he quickly told her he would replace it. On the way to her
car he told her he wanted to see her soon in Memphis, and at
that time he wanted her to tell him what was troubling her. He
thought perhaps he could help.

Lucy tried to forget him, but he didn't let her. He met her
at the Memphis airport, took her to the hotel, and told her he
would return in an hour; he had a surprise for her. He returned,
and they headed out of town. When Lucy asked where they
were going he told her she had to wait for the surprise. They
drove deep into the countryside. Finally he stopped at the foot
of a grassy hill. He took her hand, and they walked to the top
of the hill. Elvis said, "This is the surprise; my gift to you." He
pointed to a breathtaking sunset. He told her only God can
make a sunset, and that each one is an original. Then he told
her, "This one is yours Lucy." Wow, there he goes again....
being a romantic. They kissed and ran back to the car. Elvis
laid out a picnic lunch. He told Lucy that one day when he
was upset he went for a drive, and ended up at this spot. Elvis
thought this was the most beautiful place in the world. He took
in the beauty of the place, and felt close to God, and since that
time he came often to talk and to pray; always alone because
he had not met anyone he wanted to share it with....until he
met her.
He told Lucy he had met some musicians, and thought
they could help each other if they hooked up. He had made a

record for his mama, and was soon gonna do more now that he had graduated. Then he told her she would be real proud of him in a year.

He was determined he was going to 'make it.' Lucy agreed, and told him he was going to be sensational. She had been praying for him; she knew God was listening because he always listens. Elvis was moved that Lucy had faith in him. He wanted Lucy to be a part of his success, and wanted her to help him. To do so, she thought she would have to live a double life filled with deception and lies, and it was not in her nature. She told him she wanted to be a part of his life, but pleaded with him to promise he would give her time, and not ever tell anyone about her. They sat in silence for awhile before he told her he sometimes felt she was going to disappear. He thought their moments together were so great because there weren't going to be many. He thought his career was going to start moving very fast, and he didn't want the important things to get left behind. That is why he couldn't wait to tell her how much he loved her. He couldn't delay any longer.

Up until this point she had never willingly allowed a man to touch her. She felt like a virgin....but wasn't. She walked to the car. When she returned Elvis handed her a bouquet of wild flowers. He asked Lucy if she knew what marriage was. He answered before she could. "It's when two people give themselves to each other, and promise to love one another forever. No matter what happens. No matter who tries to stop them, they'll love each other forever." Lucy thought she would never be able to marry him. This was the best and worst moment of her life. Elvis told her he wanted them to be together forever. With her at his side he could do anything, and then he said, "Lucy honey, will you marry me?"

Lucy vowed to love him and to marry him....in the eyes of God. She told him he would be hers forever, and no matter what came between them she would love him forever. Elvis told her that he accepted her as his wife, and that he would love her and only her. He vowed that no matter what happens he would love her forever. He asked Lucy to close her eyes for a moment. He then presented her with another red rose. He told her the rose contained all the love they had promised, and that it stands for all the love he would have for her forever. He told her whenever she sees a rose let it always remind her of him. They knelt on the blanket, and Elvis asked if he could have her for his own. Lucy answered him with the first passionate kiss she had ever given. For the first time in her life she gave herself freely to a man she had chosen. Lucy said Elvis elevated her from a degraded child to a woman who knew the ecstasy of submission. As they looked up at the stars, Elvis told her that their love was written on the wind in heaven. Their vows of marriage were unofficial in the eyes of the law, but time would be the proof that it was not simply a 'teenage love.'

Elvis was determined to prove to Lucy what he could do with his career choice as a singer. Lucy told him he didn't need to prove anything to her. She told him God would always guide him, and she asked him to promise he would never leave Him out of his life. He then told Lucy he would promise if she promised him not to let anything separate them. Lucy avoided making that promise. He told her he would place his hand over his ear when he performed as a signal that he was thinking of her.

Lucy knew she had to tell him about the dark side of her life even though she knew he would be devastated, but she couldn't deal with her situation any longer. It would only be worse if she delayed any longer. When she saw him she told him she had a story to tell him about an eleven year old girl who lived in a convent. One day her grandmother told her a deal was made for her to become someone's wife. He was forty-five to fifty. The girl could do nothing about it. After they were married she tried to get away. The man abused her sexually and physically. He often hit her, and didn't stop until he saw blood. He had a family somewhere, so he was gone for months at a time, but she never knew when he would return, and besides he hired a woman to keep an eye on her. She had to follow instructions, or she would suffer the consequences. She went to a Priest for help; he told her she was immature, and to go home, and be a good wife. If she couldn't get help from the church who could she turn to for help? The young girl was told if she caused any problems her mama would be removed from the nice home she had been provided, and would have to go back to cleaning homes. She had lived a comfortable lifestyle before the little girls daddy died of tuberculosis. As was custom among French people the house was burned to the ground. The little girl was only three at the time, but that is her first memory. Somehow his mama, the mean, hateful, and hurtful, grandmother of the little girl took all the valuables before the house was destroyed. The little girl, her six siblings and mama were left destitute. Before the little girl's father died he told her she was going to be a great singer. One day she remembered her father's words about her destined to be a great singer, so she began using her voice to learn how to sing. She often was asked to sing for visitors and small groups. She had developed into a beautiful child. She was dressed to look much older than she was, and her grandmother told her she would be singing to some very important people. A day or two later she was told about the deal.'

They sat in silence for a moment; suddenly Elvis understood. His first reaction was one of despair. He sat with his head in his hands; his eyes were watery. And then he became 'unglued.' He shot up from where he had been setting, and started hitting the wall with his fist. "No, No, No," he shouted. He hugged Lucy, and they cried in each other's arms. Elvis held her tight, and told her she belonged to him. He paced the room. He told Lucy he would take care of her. Nothing had changed. He loved her and wanted to be with her; nothing else mattered.

Lucy knew Elvis couldn't afford to support a family. She also knew if he was to have any chance at success he had to be free to pursue it. She couldn't burden him when he needed to pour his energy and money into his career. When he stopped pacing he kissed Lucy. Their love had survived the first shocking revelation, but there was more to follow.

Elvis wanted Lucy to see his birthplace and where he grew up. On the drive Lucy told him she had two daughters. They were silent for a moment or two before he smiled and told her it was okay because he loved kids. He asked their age, and when Lucy replied, five and almost two, he was so sorry Lucy had to live such a horrible life.

Elvis told her she was a part of him no matter where he went or what he did. He wanted her with him, and he wanted her to meet his folks. Lucy wanted him to meet her mama too, but said they should continue to keep their love for each other a secret until things got better. They talked about having children. They spent the evening planning her escape and their future. She reminded him of the time he told her she was his 'lady in waiting.' Then she told him he was her El Lancelot, and that the E. L. stood for everlasting love.

Lucy filed for a divorce. Two days later the man appeared with the divorce papers, and as he did every time they were together he raped and beat her. The man somehow found out about the 'kook with the sideburns' and he was going to kill him dead. He grabbed the picture of Jesus from the wall, and threw it to the floor. It was surrounded with tiny pieces of broken glass. The man yelled, "He can't help you. He doesn't even exist." And he stormed out of the room.

It's amazing how quickly time passes sometimes. Lucy says she was in a daze for a few weeks, and she quit taking Elvis's calls at work. She lost a lot of weight, and wasn't feeling well. One night at the modeling studio she became dizzy and fainted. The doctor told her she had a damaged cervix and ovary. He was livid and asked Lucy, once again, to tell him the situation she was in, but she refused to talk about it. When the doctor told her she wouldn't survive much more of this treatment she told him she had filed for a divorce. The doctor was willing to help her if only she would let him. Lucy was sick to learn she was pregnant because she knew it was the result of the rape. The surgery was performed the following day. She lost half of an ovary, but the baby was saved.

Lucy loved her children, but despised their father. Depression took over and she nearly jumped from a window. Her neighbors arrived to stop her just in time. When she was released from the hospital she received a call from her attorney; good news at last. Her neighbor had filed for a legal order that prevented the Man from coming there. Additionally, the Man was required to provide a larger home. One month later she moved into a beautiful home in an exclusive neighborhood. She no longer had anyone watching her.

Elvis continued to call, but she didn't want him in Monroe. She was certain the Man would kill him. She certainly didn't want to take the risk.

Her baby was born late in July, 1954. Lucy often thought of Elvis. The Presley's didn't have a phone at that time, but he had given her a neighbor's number. One afternoon Lucy was shocked and excited to hear Elvis's voice coming out of the radio. He was singing, 'That's alright 'Mama.' She was so happy for him she started to cry. It hurt her that she couldn't be with him to enjoy his accomplishment. Soon there were more songs, and after a year he got on the Louisiana Hayride. He was definitely on his way to success.

One late spring afternoon Lucy took Denise to the park. She noticed someone in the distance walking in her direction. She was frightened, and tried to grab Denise, but she playfully ran from her. By the time she had her in her arms she was shocked to see it was Elvis. He asked her if she was happy to see him as he stretched out his arms. She put Denise down and ran to him. They embraced, and it was a moisture moment. Elvis crouched to play with Denise who was holding onto Lucy's leg. He asked Lucy if she was his. She said that she wasn't, but wished that she was. Then she brought him up to date. She told him he should go on with his life. He told her not to be foolish. He reminded her that their love was forever, and nothing else mattered. He told Lucy he would like to put the Man out of his misery. Once again Lucy told him to get those thoughts out of his mind because she would lose him for sure, and he would destroy his dream. He asked her to travel with him, but she declined. She told him when he had climbed all the mountains there were to climb she would be with him if he still wanted her. He assured her he would always want her, and that he keeps meeting new girls, but none come close to her. Lucy knew Elvis was human, and his image was important. She told him he didn't need to worry about what she heard. She understood, and would always be there for him; no matter what.

He told her there was some guy who wanted to promote him, and after talking about it a while he asked Lucy to tell him what she thought. She asked some questions, and realized he wanted it, so she asked him what was stopping him from signing with the colonel. She told him she would love to see him on the big screen. She advised him not to sign for more than two years, so that when he was a complete success he could take back control of his life. He asked her if she needed money. She lied, and said she didn't. Before he headed on to Memphis Lucy promised to accept his calls. Less than two weeks later a dozen red roses were delivered to her at work. The card read, 'Love Is Forever – El Lancelot.' The following day he called from Texas. He asked if she remembered telling him to look right at the audience, and give them all he had. She said that she did. Then he replied, "Well, it's workin', baby!"

Lucy learned from her boss that Elvis was to perform in Monroe. She hurried to get her work done, and rushed out the door and down the street. As she turned the corner there stood Elvis holding a red rose. He asked her to do him the honor of walking with him. When she asked why he didn't call he told her he liked to see her face light up when he surprised her. They went to a movie; 'Desiree.' It was a moving story that reminded them of their love. Desiree was Napoleon's lost love. His career and great ambition forced them apart, but their love never died. They discussed the movie when it was over. Elvis told her she would always be his Desiree, and that

Napoleon was a fool to let her go. Then he promised he would never make that mistake.

It had been two years since she saw him perform at the Eagles Nest, and now she would be in the audience once again. When Elvis appeared the crowd went wild. Lucy said he was sensational, and she was so proud to know him. They met afterwards; Elvis wanted to hear her thoughts about the show.

He signed exclusively with the colonel, and immediately was off to Hollywood for a screen test. April 1956, his career skyrocketed beyond anything imagined. He began calling Lucy more often giving her little details about what he was doing. He would profess his love, and ask her to join him, but she was still married, and didn't want to be seen. She couldn't bear involving him in a scandal, and the media was following every move he made. When she read that he might be going into the service she talked with him about it. At the time he knew very little about it. A week later she was surprised to receive mail from him; it was a first. She was a bit irritated because he sent her five thousand dollars. She told him she didn't want his money. He told her to buy a wardrobe of peach colored clothes, and added that everything he had was hers. He promised never to send money again. A few days later she received two beautiful dresses. She told him not to send anything. All she wanted from him was to see him in person. He asked her again to make a trip to see him. She again told him it was too risky.

When Lucy turned twenty-one she met Elvis in Memphis. He was now twenty-three. She wondered if they had outgrown their teenage love. He was no longer the unknown country boy she fell in love with. She would quickly learn nothing had changed, unless it was possible to love each other even more. He told her he thought he would die if she wasn't in his life, and once again he asked her why she couldn't be with him permanently. It didn't need to be discussed. They both knew

the answer. He asked her if she remembered that he told her
he would cover an ear when he performed as a signal that he
was thinking of her. He decided he would now stretch out his
arm in the air. He told her whenever she saw him raise his
arm it would be a signal that he would never forget her....not
ever.

He told her about Graceland and hoped she would live
there with him one day. The street was named 'Bellevue' at
the time. He took that as a sign it was meant to be his because
'Bellevue' is Lucy's middle name. She wanted to keep his
spirits high, so she told him it would be wonderful, but she
knew the circumstances of her life made it unlikely. He called
her Desiree when he reminded her of the vows they made to
each other. It became his, 'pet' name for her, and she loved
it.

Elvis wanted to tell his mama about Lucy. He thought she
would be able to help. She so wanted Elvis to marry, and give
her grandchildren. But Lucy still balked. With three children she
believed no one would accept her as his family. I personally
believe his folks would have welcomed her and the children,
and would have been wonderful grandparents. In any case,
Elvis told her he would keep their secret a while longer, but
that he wanted to marry her before, 'all the Hollywood stuff
got crazy.' Lucy says Elvis was quite naïve. He didn't have a
clue that such a disclosure would create such a humongous
scandal that it would ruin his career. She did promise she
would marry him sometime. He told her he wanted to marry
her before he went into the Army.

They drove to a grassy incline overlooking a river; probably
the Mississippi. They walked together as they often did. Elvis
reached in his pocket, and pulled out a red rose and a small
box. He reminded her she had told him to only give her small
things. As he laughed he told her this was the smallest thing
he could find. Lucy was warmed that he remembered he had
promised to replace the cross lost in the grass. As always
he was romantic with his presentation. He told her the cross
symbolized their love crossed with God's love. And until she

wore his ring she was to wear it close to her heart. He told her he put all the love he could squeeze into the tiny cross.

Elvis loved to hear her speak French. In French she said, "For always, my love, my heart is yours. I love you, El Lancelot. I love you very much." She taught Elvis each word, and she was his Desiree. He told her never to change her hair. It was natural, and he loved it long and black.

Late one night, Lucy heard a sound coming from the kitchen that frightened her. The door leading from the garage was kicked in. There stood the Man...He was angry... His eyes were bulging. He lunged at Lucy as he screamed, "You little whore." There was a very sad scene that woke two of the girls. They ran into the kitchen, and pleaded with him not to hurt their mommy. He beat her very badly, but this time he didn't rape her.

He ranted and raved about Elvis. He told her if he ever saw Elvis in town again he would kill him for sure, and he didn't care how famous he was. Lucy knew the Man was capable of killing Elvis, her, and the girls.

The following day she found a new place to live, and moved in that night. She planned to leave Monroe, and not tell anyone where she was going; not even Elvis. She had to protect him too. She thought he would be better off without her because the darkness of her past had prevented them from making a life together. The papers were full of stories about his girlfriends, and she was happy for him...a bit jealous...but she knew he was the kind of man who needed someone all the time.

She gave notice at work. The following week Elvis called. He told her his basic training would be in Texas, and he wanted her to move there; he would pay for everything. He told her when he got out he wouldn't be famous anymore, and life would be as it was when they first met...and she would have no more reasons why she couldn't marry him. Could he actually believe what he was saying? She told Elvis she had something to tell him, but quickly she was haunted by the

Man's threat to kill him. She knew she had to follow through with her plans. She told him she wouldn't be in Monroe because she would be visiting relatives for a while; her aunt was sick. Elvis could have read something more into what she said, because he told her not to run away again. He begged her not to leave him again. She just had to be there when he made the trip to see her. Lucy promised him she would not run away. When she hung up the phone she sobbed because she knew different.

The stress of moving, and fearing the Man would appear, made Lucy sick to her tummy. One of the employees told her it was probably flu, and gave her a couple of pills to take. She told her they contained a small amount of quinine, and she would feel fine in a short time. The following two hours she was doubled over in pain, and was rushed to the hospital. The doctor scolded her for allowing a store clerk to medicate her. She could have killed herself....and the baby. Lucy did not know she was pregnant, nor did she suspicion it. It was a cruel twist of fate. This was a child created by the deep love she and Elvis shared. She should have been happy, but how could she be? Elvis's life was in danger, his career wouldn't survive the scandal, he was soon to enter the army, and she was still legally married.

Lucy's sister now lived in Denver. She invited Lucy to live with her until she decided what she wanted to do. Before Lucy drove out of town she cashed the five thousand dollar check Elvis gave her. She was desperately in need of money, or she would have left with it un-cashed. The girls were happy to leave their home because they associated it with leaving their mean, hateful, and hurtful daddy. Lucy drove into a tremendous snow storm. All the luggage blew off the roof, and down into a ravine. She got stuck. A stranger took them to a nearby inn. The storm didn't pass for two days. By the time Lucy could make a call the police had informed Mary they found the car empty, and said they no doubt froze to death trying to find help. A few days later they learned a man was killed in an accident a mile from the Inn that Lucy was at; it was the man who gave them a ride.

Lucy told Mary not to tell anyone they were alive. It was good that everyone thought they had perished in the storm. Their bodies couldn't be discovered until the snow melts, and then when no bodies were found....well, she would deal with that later. She hoped Elvis would 'feel' they were still alive. If not, when the time was right she would contact him.

Lucy moved into a small cabin near Grand Junction. It was a good place to hide, but it was miserably cold.

She says she cannot explain the depth of her love for her daughters. She never once associated them with the Man. They were gentle, beautiful, and strong. Lucy and her girls had actually grown up together, because Lucy was a child when they were born.

She lived in constant fear the Man would find them. He apparently didn't believe they perished in the storm because Mary told her he had been diligent in asking about her. Lucy home-schooled the girls so they wouldn't get behind in their schooling. She hoped Elvis's military hitch would pass fast. She had faith in God, and knew he wouldn't desert her.

Lucy returned to Alexandria to visit her mama who was ill. Her mama recovered; Lucy stayed. The baby was born August 23, 1958. She had long dark hair that flowed almost to her shoulders. Lucy immediately saw Elvis in her eyes. She named her, 'Desiree Presley,' and knew her daddy would be pleased. She returned to work, and was blessed to find good jobs. Her mama watched the girls when she was away.

Darn...Darn...Darn the media. Several people, whose job it was to report the news, did a tremendous disservice to Elvis and Lucy. I suppose they couldn't possibly know, but they surely knew they were putting out stories they did not know were true. Lucy had waited for Elvis to return from Germany, and now it was reported that Priscilla was the only girl he had ever loved. Lucy was overwhelmed with mixed emotions.

Around this time her boss called her into his office. Business was slow. Lucy expected to lose her job. Jack asked her to set. He was emotionless. What happened next was absolutely bizarre. He told Lucy it was the proper time in his life to marry and have children. He didn't believe in love, but he felt if two people can work together, a marriage will succeed. He had evaluated her situation, and it was obvious she needed someone to help raise her children. Lucy was angry, but she had her job to think about, so she suppressed her feelings. She reminded Jack that she was still married, but only because she didn't have the three hundred fifty dollars to pay for it. He offered to pay for it, but once again she declined. How on earth could she marry him? They had never been on a date. In fact, there had never been an indication he had a personal interest in her. Theirs had been a business relationship from the very beginning. He told her to 'think about it' and 'dismissed' her. This was definitely bizarre.

When Elvis returned he gave a TV press conference; Lucy watched. I watched it too and I remember it well. When Elvis was asked if there was someone he especially wanted to see he quickly placed his hand to his ear. Lucy knew it was a tape, so she rushed to the phone, full of excitement, and called Graceland. He wasn't home, and she didn't leave a message. She called several times only to get a busy signal. She finally quit calling. The thought of rejection, and having him confirm the news was true was too much for her. She couldn't bear it; she was determined to put him out of her mind. I was so disappointed at her decision, and the turn of events.

She kept apprised of the news; Elvis's career was on the rise. The colonel was certainly behind it. Already there was an album, a movie, and a television special. Elvis was back on top, and his every move was being watched.

In the meantime, Jack was content to give Lucy all the time she needed to evaluate his offer. He had loved once, and she ran off and married someone else. Since that time he had an extremely sad outlook. What a waste. Lucy invited him to her place for dinner. After dinner he increased his offer. He told Lucy he had purchased a large ranch style house in Alexandria's most prestigious suburb for her, and she could move in whenever she wanted. Lucy was tempted, but she declined. Jack was well-groomed, nice-looking, had good manners, and didn't appear to be violent. Lucy thought he was definitely a good catch if you wanted a loveless marriage, but she loved Elvis. How could she possibly accept Jack's offer? But, there was one thing they had in common. They had both been scarred by love, and they didn't expect to love again.

Lucy told Jack about her previous marriage, and included the fact that the Man could very well appear in her life again. She warned him he was capable of anything, including violence. Finally, she saved the money for her divorce. She made a quick trip to Monroe, the place that held her best and worst memories; Elvis and the Man. Her slavery had lawfully ended. Before she returned to Alexandria she went to all the places Elvis had taken her. She cried a lot, but it was good for her to relive the memories.

It was market time in Dallas. Jack traveled with Lucy this time. He thought it was time for him to learn about the business he owned. He was an oil man before he went into the boutique business. During break Lucy picked up a magazine. She read that Priscilla was Elvis's bride to be.' She tried to digest what she had read. During lunch Jack asked her if she had given any thought to his offer. Lucy said in a sarcastic tone, "why not?"

He replied, "How about right now?" Lucy was startled that he would marry her with no prior plans. She was vulnerable. Her dreams of being with Elvis were shattered. She felt rejected. The thought returned that even if she could work it out with Elvis the colonel would not allow them to be together. Lucy's brains were scrambled. She thought a marriage to Jack would at least give her children a home and a secure future. Lucy decided marrying Jack would be a new beginning that would end her hurts of the past.

Jack quickly found a judge. At the courthouse the license bureau clerk requested proof that Lucy was old enough; she was twenty-four. She wondered why it wasn't requested thirteen years earlier. Lucy was so dazed the judge had to tell her she was supposed to say, 'I do.' She hesitated because she was thinking of Elvis; she had to let him go. She said, "I do."

Lucy's troubles never let up. Jack made no attempt to introduce her or the children to any of his family or friends; not even his parents. She asked Jack why he wanted to get married, and he told her it was the only way he could have her. It was clear there would not be any giving or receiving love in this marriage. Jack told Lucy she had forfeited her salary by marrying him. Now she was in a loveless marriage, and had no money of her own.

Two months later she was pregnant. Jack welcomed the news; he wanted a son. Lucy was devastated. There was little joy in having a child under the circumstances of her marriage, but Jacques was born shortly before Desiree's birthday.

Her mama was ill again and wanted to see her. Lucy arrived just in time. Her mama was alert and clear headed. She kissed Desiree and Jacques, and told them to go play in the sunshine. A nurse took them out of the room as she asked Lucy to set beside her. Holding Lucy's hand, she told her to tell Desiree's father not to wait. And then she asked Lucy if she would tell him for her. Lucy promised, and her mama smiled, closed her eyes, and passed on.

When Lucy returned to Dallas she went to work in a public relations position at a very nice hotel with a considerable increase in pay. Elvis was in the news much of the time, and his music was everywhere too. She realized she had not given him a chance to decide what to do about them. And all this time Elvis thought Lucy and the children had died in the snow storm, but he had to look for her; he had to know how they died.

Lucy took courses in Christian Theology that led to certification a year later. She studied voice and opera for her enjoyment. She began teaching Desiree piano when she was only four; she was a fast learner. Desiree was growing into an extraordinary child and her personality was becoming more like her daddy's. Lucy felt sad when she called her, Desiree, so when she started to school Lucy asked her if she would mind using her middle name. Desiree said it was okay so after that she was Romaine or Rome.

Jack was busy with his own life and grew distant. He complained about expenses. Lucy was working and making a good salary, so she made sure he paid nothing. Shame on him! The relationship lacked affection and fulfillment, but the children had a happy home, so Lucy endured it. At least it was an improvement compared to the Man.

Early in 1965 Lucy was pregnant with her sixth child. Jack apologized and told her it would never happen again....and it didn't. Lucy asked him for a divorce a number of times, but he always refused her request. He told her he would never allow her to disgrace him. Lucy's last child, a girl, was born in September.

Priscilla was living at Graceland. Lucy had not seen or talked to Elvis for eight years. She said by now she cried only once or twice a month instead of every day, but she was still in love with him. In 1967, she enrolled in paralegal courses and volunteered as an entertainment coordinator for the International Visitors Program.

Lucy was deeply hurt when she learned Elvis married Priscilla. She couldn't forget the memory of the boy on the hill who vowed to love her...and only her....forever, but she prayed he was happy.

She changed jobs again. She was slowly working her way up the ladder to success and a great salary. She soon had a huge opportunity to sing at a scheduled engagement in Acapulco, but Jack wouldn't allow her to go. They had a bitter argument. He believed an upswing in her musical career would be a downswing in her morals. Lucy knew it would be her last chance to pursue the dream she wanted since she was a child. Once again she was not in control of her life.

Less than three months after Elvis married someone had sent her fourteen peach-colored talisman roses. The card read, 'True love never dies.' Why was there fourteen instead of the usual twelve? And then she remembered she met Elvis in 1953 and now it was 1967; fourteen years. Could they be from Elvis? The following day Lucy answered the phone. Her "hello" was met with a long silence. The voice made her tremble.

"Is this Lucy?"

"Yes, who is this?" There was another long silence, and then she heard a dial tone. Elvis discontinued the call without another word. What an emotional time that must have been for them. Had they not talked with each other for so long they couldn't recognize each other's voice? That night Lucy couldn't sleep, and work was extremely difficult.

When he called again he told her he had just found out that she and the children were alive. He was happy, but it was an emotional shock for him. He was pleading to see her; Los Angeles or Dallas would be okay. He asked if he could call her the following morning at ten. The phone rang promptly at ten. He wanted to see her that very day. They agreed to meet Wednesday in Los Angeles. Elvis told her when he was told she died in a snowstorm it nearly killed him.

I imagine they were near exhaustion by the time he knocked on her door. The moment was at hand. Lucy says when she heard a light knock on the door she knew the only man she had ever loved stood on the other side. When she opened the door and saw him she was awestruck for a moment. He was the best-looking man she had ever seen. He was magnificent. They stood and looked at each other ever so long. Lucy was no longer sixteen years old, and he was no longer eighteen wearing the oversized baggy pants. After a lingering hug and a few tears they talked.

Elvis thought he would never see her again. He used to lie awake, and wonder how she had died. In his search for her some people told him they heard she had run off with some singer. He knew that wasn't right because he was the singer. The Man must have blown off his mouth many times, but I doubt people took him serious. He called before going to Germany, and after he returned. If only Lucy would have called him. If only she had talked to him. It is said, 'There's a reason for everything.' Perhaps so, but it certainly is difficult for me to understand sometimes. Then he heard she married a Texas oilman. He was hurt, and tried to hate her, but he was excited to hear she was alive. When he started to tell Lucy about Priscilla she said it wasn't necessary, but he needed to. A friend brought this little girl over one day, and Elvis was shocked because she looked so much like her. Lucy tried to stop him, but he told her she must listen to him. He continued. He was attracted to her because she reminded him more and more of Lucy. His mama was gone, he was lonely, the girl liked him...the person; not the star. He used to moan at night, and cry himself to sleep. He needed someone. He was devastated that he couldn't find Lucy. The girls in Hollywood were not who he wanted. The girl in Germany was all he had. When she arrived in Memphis he couldn't get himself to marry her. He kept thinking of Lucy. He got trapped. The colonel suddenly arranged for them to get married. Her parents were angry Elvis had not married her. He did care for her, and he again told Lucy he still thought she was dead. They sat in silence for a long while....not knowing what to say. I thought it strange that during his whole conversation he never once said Priscilla; he referred to her as 'the girl.'

Lucy told him it was time to listen to her story. She finished by telling him now that they have found each other there is another change; their marriages. Lucy told him to pretend she had died, and to forget her. He had to stand by his wife because she was pregnant. When Lucy told him it was the best thing, Elvis jumped up and yelled, "No it's not." He was still in love with Lucy. He couldn't let her go now that he finally found her. He finally felt alive again. Elvis reminded her he had told her if they were ever separated he would talk to her through his songs. He asked why she hadn't listened. They talked about the many times he had asked her advice and now he told her she helped him a lot because he remembered and followed it. When asked about Priscilla he told Lucy she was restless and uncertain. She hadn't adapted to his life. Then he asked Lucy to tell him more about her. He was impressed that she taught Sunday school to teenagers. He said he would like to teach people about God. I believe he has and possibly still does.

Lucy told him she remained married because of the children. Elvis wanted to take care of them, but once again Lucy wouldn't let him do anything that could lead news hounds to her and ruin his career. He worried that she would disappear again. She said she was through running. She told him they had to accept their destiny and be happy. Elvis replied that he could not accept anything other than being together. Lucy said something that I think is beautiful. She told Elvis 'their lives crossed, their love is written and no one can erase it.' She continued…'he helped her when she needed help by giving her so many wonderful memories. The memories had sustained her.' She added that 'memories cannot hold a person. They don't hug or keep you warm. They can't make love.' Elvis told her he had tried to live without her, and he was tired of it, but he would pray about it, and let God decide for them

They had lots of years to cover, so they continued talking. Elvis said those around him think they know him, but he keeps things from them that he would never tell them. He told her he would like to start over. When he reached the top it wasn't fun anymore. One day he thought about the time they were riding horses at the zoo, and so he bought a ranch. It was a nice place, but once he realized why he bought it…it no longer interested him…because she wasn't there. Lucy told him their love had given her something very special, and someday when they had a few hours she would tell him about it. She scooted him out the door saying she thought they would be missing him. He made sure Lucy had his phone numbers, and told her she could always reach his Uncle Vester. Lucy changed to an earlier flight. Elvis called her and told her he wanted to give her some money. She told him there wasn't any room for the exchange of money in their lives. Elvis cracked up and said, "I ain't asking for any from you, baby."

Elvis wasn't happy, and he knew Lucy wasn't either. He didn't want to delay his divorce any longer. Lucy told him he couldn't do that to Priscilla because she was pregnant. Elvis said he was tired of people telling him what he could and could not do. What he had to sing, who he had to marry, what movie he could or couldn't do, and what he can or can't do with his life. Lucy understood, but told him it simply wouldn't look right for him to divorce Priscilla while she was pregnant, and to divorce her at all could hurt his career. At this point Elvis didn't care whether he had a career. Lucy told him to please be patient; things will change. They agreed they would place themselves on their hill in Memphis when things became unbearable

One night Desiree ran out of the bedroom. She asked Lucy if her nose looked like a man's. Lucy told her it didn't, but that sometimes little girls do take on their father's features. She added she looked like her father. Desiree pointed to her nose, and told her this isn't my dad's. Lucy thought a trip to the bedroom might shed some light on Desiree's concern. She was shocked to see posters of Elvis all over the walls. The children were silent, and starred at Lucy. Desiree asked what was wrong, and then asked if she liked him. She told Lucy his name, and said a guy at school passed out tons of the posters. She asked Lucy if she had ever heard of him. Lucy told the children she wasn't born in a cave. Lucy was numb when Desiree said, "Denise said I have the same nose he does, and he's a man." Lucy tried to stay calm. She told them that Elvis was so handsome that she wouldn't mind looking like him. Everyone laughed except her sixteen year old. Melody continued to stare at Lucy until she felt very uncomfortable. Lucy was worried because Melody was quite perceptive.

Elvis met Lucy at the Memphis airport; in disguise. When they entered the hotel room he asked her to set down and listen to him. He began by telling her ever since their talk in Beverly Hills he had tried to do what she asked him too. He had tried to make Priscilla happy and be happy himself. He had made Priscilla dye her hair, so she would look more like Lucy. He even made her dress like Lucy. He had her take French lessons, so she could speak to him in French like Lucy did. He had tried to re-create Lucy, but it didn't work. Priscilla was nothing like her. He didn't learn Lucy was alive until after he was married. He told her he always wanted Lucy to have his baby. He told Lucy he knew that she would love him even if he were nothing but a hick. Lucy came close to telling him about Desiree, but she couldn't for the same reason she always had. She hoped she was doing the right thing. He sang, 'Are you Lonesome Tonight?' to her, and they talked about the times they sang together, and about his choice of songs with her in mind. He hoped she would always hear them, and know he was talking to her.

Elvis told Lucy the doctor gave him a prescription to help him function better. He needed it to get him going, and to help with his moods. His mama worried that he would get caught up in show business, and he was angry because he did. Priscilla was seeing someone else, and it troubled him. He said Priscilla was a cold woman. Perhaps because she had feelings for another or perhaps Elvis didn't give her the right kind of attention. In any case, it was clear their marriage left a lot to be desired. Lucy suggested he sweep her off her feet again. When she asked him what he really wanted from his career he told her more than anything he wanted to teach others what it is like to love God. More than once he had talked about his love for God, and that he wanted to teach others.

He seemed to need to justify their feelings. Lucy worried about the consequences of 'double adultery.' Elvis thought they were fooling themselves; his wife was cheating on him, and Lucy was in a loveless marriage. Once again he told Lucy she didn't have to remain married because he could work it out. Their love was real, so why shouldn't they be together. Their desire for each other was fulfilled once again.

It seems to me that whenever Elvis faced a crisis of any kind he called Lucy. And the times it appeared most crucial he had a need to be with her. This was a pattern that would continue through August 17, 1977.

I learned an interesting thing from reading this book. We know Priscilla reminded Elvis of Lucy, and he tried to make her a replica of Lucy. He said he didn't want to marry Priscilla because he so desperately wanted to find Lucy. Lucy is who he wanted and needed. We know he said the colonel forced him into the marriage. Did he really? Now we know the rest of the story. The Air Force Special Services noncom who introduced Priscilla to Elvis in Germany told what happened. He had put his honor on the line when he went to bat for Elvis so Colonel Beaulieu would consent to Priscilla living with Elvis in Memphis. When he heard, through the Memphis Mafia grapevine, Priscilla might be on the way out he felt obligated to inform her father of the situation. He was already aware that Elvis was content to string her along forever. It was clear he did not want to marry her. However, Elvis had a big problem. He had made many promises to Priscilla's parents including one that he would marry her. Colonel Beaulieu was livid. He called Elvis, and reminded him of his promises. He threatened him with charges of child molestation and statutory rape. He met Priscilla when she was only fourteen, and she was sixteen when she went to him in Memphis. Elvis refused to back down. Colonel Parker knew Priscilla's father wasn't bluffing. Colonel Parker took control and arranged the quick wedding;

Their marriage was doomed from the beginning. But they did a pretty good job fooling the people into believing it was a 'Cinderella' love story. At the time the noncom told his story he regretted telling Colonel Beaulieu about the situation. If he had known the anguish Priscilla would cause Elvis he never would have informed her father of the situation. He had given his word, but he would have much rather suffered the consequences of Elvis's actions.

I also learned that Elvis was told of Priscilla's infidelities from the beginning, and he was asked what he wanted to do about it. He was indifferent, and told the informant to do nothing. He commented there was a whole wide world for Priscilla to learn about, and if she gets hurt it would be a lesson for her. Perhaps he wanted to give her enough rope to hang herself. And perhaps he thought she deserved some of the freedom he had.

He called Lucy after he decided to perform in Vegas. He was both excited and nervous. He was working hard; everything had to be perfect. He wanted Lucy's advice on his wardrobe. He remembered Lucy telling him he needed to be different… more like Liberace…but more masculine, and suited to his personal style. He wanted Lucy to be in the audience, but she didn't promise to be there. She told him he was going to be magnificent, and reminded him of her premonition. He hadn't forgotten, and said it had sustained him many times.

When Lucy arrived in Vegas she was startled to see the city looked like a carnival called 'Elvis land.' Posters of him were everywhere; some life size, others three times larger. Lucy learned the show was sold out. But a 'skuzzy' person quickly appeared and agreed to sell her a ticket for all the cash she had; twenty dollars…five dollars more than the ticket price. She went into the ladies room to change clothes and found a picture of Elvis on the underside of the toilet seat cover. She went into the coffee shop to kill time, and Elvis stared at her when she opened the menu. The colonel had thought of everything. She hoped to let Elvis know that she was there, but when she called she was told he wasn't taking any calls. She left a message; wish him luck from Desiree. Lucy was seated in the back. It wasn't her choice, but she was happy to get in. From the moment Elvis appeared the crowd went wild. Lucy listened to him sing several songs and by the time he finished, 'Are You Lonesome Tonight,' she was in tears. He was back on top, and she was so happy for him. But once again his fame and her situation would always stand in the way of their love. It was too much for her. She left the auditorium, and went directly to the airport.

He was angry when he learned he was not given her message. He told her he would be going to Europe, but first he had to clear up some things, and he hated it that Lisa was in the middle.

He recorded another song for her; this one was, 'snowbird.' This time he didn't have a red rose for Lucy. Instead he gave her a yellow porcelain rose, and told her to put it on her dresser to forever remind her of his love. He spoke again of making their relationship permanent, and for the first time Lucy thought it was possible.

The following month she received the usual dozen roses for her thirty-fourth birthday only this time the inscription on the card was different; 'you're my snowbird.'

A week or so before Christmas she met Elvis in Washington DC. He was registered at the Washington Hotel under the name of Colonel Burrows. He was traveling alone. Traveling alone was uncommon for him. I wonder if he enjoyed those moments, and somehow had a sense of 'freedom.' He so wanted what they had when they first met. They had plans and dreams of spending their life together. He wondered what happened; where had all the years gone? Lucy told him their love was real, and would not change, but his family and friends would most likely destroy her if they knew. He assured her he would change that one day.

He had a new dream. He wanted to clean house and start a production company, and he wanted Lucy to be a part of it. He wanted Lucy to help him gain control of his life. He also wanted to write his biography. He wanted people to know she was very much a part of it. He told her every woman he was attracted to was a version of her. They discussed his desire to work with the narcotics bureau; he wanted to become an undercover agent like his friend, John O'Grady. Elvis gave Lucy an envelope and told her not to open it until she arrived home. It contained seven thousand dollars. She thought of Desiree, and decided to keep it. She splurged, and used much of it for ballet and piano lessons. I think Elvis would have liked that.

Elvis called periodically the following year. He was touring and performing in Vegas. Lucy resigned herself to enjoy the moments they had, and to handle their separation. After talking they of course knew their love was strong. He told Lucy he felt better just hearing her voice. He didn't want his life; he never did. He reminded her it could have been different from the start; when they first met. But it wasn't doing either of them any good to dwell on what could have been; because from the start Lucy felt she had to protect Elvis and his career. Lucy prayed that God would protect him and never leave his side.

When he called again he wished they could go off together, and leave everything behind. He wanted to quit taking drugs, but he couldn't. He hurt all over, and the drugs didn't help. Lucy told him she would go with him to the Mayo Clinic, or wherever he wanted to go. Lucy had a difficult time accepting he was addicted.

He made reservations for Lucy Jones in Los Angeles. He talked more about the drugs and how he had to have them to keep going. Lucy told him the drugs were the cause of his problems....not the solution. He told her he never wanted any of 'this' to harm her. He told her he wanted more than anything for them to be together; he always had, and he still did. He asked Lucy to pray with him. She was thrilled he still had his faith in God; they knelt and prayed.

The next few times he called he talked about his problems; how unhappy he was. He did not bring up the drug situation. Then he didn't call for several months which left Lucy with nothing to do but quietly worry about him. When he started the calls again it was basically the same thing. They spoke of their love for each other. He wanted to buy a house near Disneyworld where they would live one day. They knew living at Graceland was out of the question, because there were too many bad memories there. He said living in Texas would be nice also, and asked her to start looking for a house.

Elvis wrote a poem and dedicated it to Lucy. In it he referred to her as his greatest treasure. It was only nine lines, but it was enough to tell Lucy what their love meant to him. He also enclosed a check for two thousand dollars, and told her to get a small gift. It seems absurd to me that the Presley Estate controls Elvis's letters and copyrights, and therefore would not give permission for Lucy's poem to appear in her book. For Pete's sake it's hers. Elvis wrote it to her, and sent it to her. It seems she could do whatever she wants to with it. After all it is Desiree's legacy. The poem was valued at one hundred thousand dollars in 1988. I believe she still has it.

He called again in March from Monroe. That must have dredged up lots of memories; good and bad. The following day he called from North Carolina. The Colonel had Elvis performing in many small towns. Lucy knew he would be a sellout wherever he performed, and wondered why he wasn't entertaining in Japan, Germany, or France. Months earlier he had said he had a desire to do so. He continued to call from all the places he performed. Lucy sent him a birthday present for his fortieth birthday. She thought he may need a lift. Perhaps he did. Turning forty didn't bother me, but it sure does many people. He called a few weeks later, and thanked her and asked her to meet him in Memphis. She was determined to tell him about Desiree. Many times she intended too, but something always happened to make her hold back. Now she worried if she had done the right thing. Desiree was seventeen, and had developed into a beautiful girl like her mama, and yet she looked so much like her daddy.

A few days later he called and wanted to know when she was going to meet him; he needed to be with her. He asked if she remembered when he named her Desiree; she did and she quoted the words of love that he spoke at that time. He asked if she still believed no one would ever destroy their love, and she did. The following day he called to tell her he had made the reservation for her to fly to Memphis the next day. He was determined someone in the family was going to meet her, so they drove to Graceland; she met his Uncle Vester. Lucy couldn't accept the invite to go inside, so Elvis told his Uncle Vester they were going for a drive. They went to 'their' hill where they had said their marriage vows twenty-two years earlier. Elvis told her he was nothing without her, and that all the other women were nothing more than a human need. It was never love like it was with them. He told Lucy that even though he was lonely he had known his greatest happiness with her. And he needed to know that she believed he belonged to her and no one else. When she told him she did he placed a ring on her finger. It had a large diamond in the center, and was surrounded by diamond baguettes. Lucy remembered the bracelet he threw into the river many years earlier; she would never hurt him like that again.

Lucy told him that she had always dreamed of wearing a beautiful white wedding dress. He told her one day she would wear the most beautiful dress in the world. It began raining so they dashed for the car. He pulled her to him, and told her the first time they kissed was in the moonlight, they became one in the setting sun, and now he wanted to kiss her in the rain. The ring was too big for her delicate finger, and the rain made it slip off, so she placed it in his pocket as they hugged. Elvis told her he didn't want them to be separated any longer because they had already lost too many years. He was certain they belonged together. He talked about the production company that he wanted to start, and reminded Lucy he wanted her to work with him. He called later in the evening to talk more, and to see if she needed anything. Lucy remembered the ring and Elvis said he would size it for her, and give it to her the next time they were together. Before they said goodbye he told her she was going to be a part of his life real soon.

Elvis continued to pressure Lucy to visit him more often, and he wanted her to marry him. Lucy had mixed emotions. She still had three children living at home; Desiree seventeen, and two minor children, fourteen and ten. She still worried what it would do to Elvis even though he wanted to give up his singing career. She was concerned what it would do to the children to take them away from their father, and she feared the colonel's wrath. It all seemed insurmountable, and deep down I imagine Elvis had his worries and concerns even though he wanted to marry Lucy. They definitely had a dilemma. Life certainly wasn't easy for them.

In the meantime, Lucy stayed in contact with Elvis's daddy. She never told him her name, and it didn't seem to make any difference to him; they both had Elvis's welfare at heart. Vernon asked her how long she had known Elvis, and when she responded twenty-three years she quickly asked how he was doing. Vernon too was concerned about Elvis over medicating himself, and said he was going to get to the bottom of it. After a while Vernon asked if she was the person Elvis had told him would stand by him no matter what? It wasn't important for him to know her name, but he wanted to know if she was the person he could depend on when everyone else turned on him. Lucy didn't answer. She thought she was, but perhaps she wasn't. She didn't care. She simply wanted Elvis to get some help. Vernon told her he thought it was nice of her to be so concerned.

A 'friend' of Lucy's called Desiree, and told her Elvis was her father, and she thought her mother should tell her. Desiree didn't discuss it with Lucy; Lucy didn't know about it until the writing of this book. It was learned Lucy had never discussed it with the 'friend;' she simply figured it out.

Elvis was once again doing one night stands, and called frequently. He told Lucy he had a title for his biography; 'Through My Eyes.' Gosh! I think that's a great title. It's still not too late, if only he would do it. He suggested they could just disappear and write. Elvis told her all he really wants is a nice house, a few children, and a wife who truly loves him. That sounds reasonable to me. When he asked Lucy to meet him in Memphis or Los Angeles she told him she would when he finished the tour.

One day when Lucy arrived home Desiree's car was parked in the drive. She left a note in the car telling Lucy that she was going to Los Angeles, and would contact her later. She needed to be alone. A few days later one of Desiree's friends called, and told Lucy that Desiree was with her, and she would call after she got some things figured out. Lucy wondered what things she had to figure out. Many weeks passed before Desiree called her mama. She told her she was now using her rightful name; Presley. Lucy was shocked, and asked her why she changed her name. Desiree said, "Because it is my name." Lucy didn't want to discuss it over the phone.

A few days later Lucy received a call from a man who had a deep southern accent. He told her never to contact Elvis again if she valued her life. Gads! It was another reason not to tell Elvis about Desiree. The man told her not to see Elvis when he came to Dallas. Lucy didn't go to either performance. I wonder if Vernon casually mentioned Lucy to someone, but he didn't know her name, and cell phones were not heard of then. I suppose it could have been learned from Lucy's 'friend.' But the person who most likely caused the call to take place was Jack. Even though it was a loveless marriage I imagine he had no desire to be humiliated with a divorce.

Lucy was extremely troubled when Elvis told her he was now taking injections because nothing else helped. He didn't tell her the name of the medicine. She was hysterical, and begged him not to do it. He told her not to worry. It was just for this tour, and then everything would change, and then they would be together. He had to keep it up. Keep what up? I believe Elvis proved he is a great actor. I believe much of what he was doing was just that; an act to make what he was about to do on August 16, 1977 believable.

The summer passed without any phone calls from Elvis. Lucy received a dozen orange talisman roses on her fortieth birthday. This time the card read, 'Never doubt my love, El Lancelot.'

She called Vernon for an update on Elvis's condition. He sounded worried and gloomy. He told Lucy the situation was bad. He added 'they' have put someone else in his bed to watch him; her name is Sheila. It was all too mind-boggling for Lucy. Vernon promised to keep in touch.

Lucy was starting a leather fashions business, and had already scheduled a trip to Los Angeles the following month, and would see Elvis then. He asked Lucy to call him before she left; she didn't. He just couldn't understand why she was jealous. That's a man for you. And Lucy, still married, knew she was being faithful to him. But she was now anxious to get out of her loveless marriage, and still had hope that she and Elvis would be married one day. At this point in time I think she wanted to see him squirm…Just like a woman.

Elvis called a few days later. Neither one were very civil to each other. They were both hurt and it sounded like they wanted to inflict more hurt upon each other. In any case, Lucy was hurt. This was their first argument, and it was about what had always been; the frustration of not being together, and the green eyed monster had raised its ugly head on both their parts. Lucy abruptly ended the call. Elvis quickly called back, but Lucy wouldn't answer, and she instructed the children to say she wasn't home. I wonder if that teaches a child to lie.

The news reported he was engaged to a twenty year old former beauty queen. Elvis called in March from Alexandria, Louisiana. Lucy thought it ironic since Desiree was born there. He begged Lucy to listen to him. He had to talk to her. Basically he couldn't get her out of his head, and he was sorry he hurt her. He wanted to see her. The engagement wasn't for real. Lucy knew she loved him deeply, but just couldn't deal with being continually hurt by how he was living his life. He was interrupted, and said he would call again. He wasn't well, but he was going to finish the tour. She asked him to quit until he felt good again. He tried to assure her that he would be fine. He needed to know that she still believed in him, and knew that she was the only one for him for always. He had to hear her say it. She told him he was the only man she had ever loved, and she would always be his. He told her there would be more changes when the tour was over, and he prayed everything would work out as planned. Lucy put a smile on his face when she told him they still had time to grow old together, and the last years can be the best. Once again they professed their love for each other. He told her he would call her while he was on tour.

The following month a tragedy occurred. Desiree had returned to Dallas. She worked at a law firm, and was taking paralegal classes at Southern Methodist University. She and Lucy were no longer close, and that hurt Lucy a bunch; and probably Desiree. I can identify with that. It hurts for a very long time, but all they can do is pick up the pieces, and allow love to sustain them. Lucy was on the way to a movie with a friend who was driving a convertible. The convertible overturned when a car pulling another car cut them off. Desiree was trapped underneath, and was dragged across the pavement. She arrived at the hospital in critical condition. Her blouse was burned into her chest, her cheeks were embedded with gravel, and she almost lost an arm. She couldn't move one hand, and she wondered if it would heal. I imagine she was concerned whether she would ever be able to play the piano again. Elvis was not well, but continued his schedule, so Lucy prayed for both of them.

Mid-June Elvis performed in Omaha, Nebraska. I believe it was Father's day. I had tried to get tickets, but was told it was sold out. Several years later I learned it wasn't. In any case, I would have had to drive all night in order to be at work Monday morning. It is said that when Elvis announced he was going to sing, 'Are You Lonesome Tonight? He looked down and said, "I am and I was."

About three weeks later Lucy received a collect call from John Jones. She knew he must be at Graceland. He was worried because he couldn't reach her. She told him about Desiree's accident without mentioning her name. He was sorry Lucy had to go through it alone. Lisa would be with him until he left on the sixteenth. Elvis told Lucy they could not let anyone come between them, and then he asked her if she was ready to face it, and blow their minds. He told her she couldn't even imagine the plans that he had. And when the tour was over they would get married like they should have a long time ago. When he asked what she thought of his plans she excitedly said, "That would be wonderful." Elvis was excited, and told her there would be no more excuses from either of them. He wanted them to get started on the book, and added they would answer those guys. He was so nervous about the book his ex-bodyguards wrote.

Before they hung up he said he hoped her 'little' girl would get well soon. Once again he asked what her name was. Lucy had avoided answering him by asking him a question, but now she was caught off guard. She told him she's not a little girl... she's eighteen, and her name is....Desiree. There was nothing but silence. Lucy said it was a silence that screamed for an explanation. Finally he told her he didn't realize she was such a big girl, and then asked why she named her Desiree. Before Lucy could say anything he wanted to know if there was something she wasn't telling him. In a low, slow, monotone she replied that it was because she liked the name. She knew she was giving herself away with every word. She told him there was so much she had to tell him. He asked why she was acting so strange, and wanted to know if anything was wrong. She didn't want to tell him over the phone, so she continued the monotone sound to avoid allowing her emotions to take over. She told him she had something to discuss with him, but it could wait.

He had to hear her say she loved him before they hung up the phone. She laughed and called him a crazy man for needing to be assured of something he already knew, without a doubt, but Lucy was happy to humor him one more time. "You know I love you Elvis Presley. I've loved you since you were eighteen. You captured my heart and it's been yours ever since. And when you grow old I'll always make you feel young. Don't feel bad about the past. It's over. Let's look ahead." She promised him she would end her loveless marriage, and marry him. And when he returned she had something wonderful to tell him, but only when they were together.

At one point Elvis repeated, 'Desiree,' and then he was silent for a moment before he said, "Aha...well I'll be darned." He thought he knew what the surprise was; he hoped what he was thinking was true. Elvis wanted Lucy to pray with him, and he said the prayer. He thanked her for giving him something to live for, and for giving him hope. He was going to call her before he left.

Lucy didn't want to miss his call so she hurried home. The phone was ringing as she rushed to grab it. It was Desiree. Lucy immediately knew something was wrong because Desiree spoke much too gentle and soft than was normal for her when she asked Lucy how she was feeling. When Lucy said that she was okay Desiree told her that Elvis Presley died. Desiree says her mama said, "Oh my G _ _", and hung up the phone. At that moment Jack appeared, and said, "Did you hear? He's dead." With that Lucy screamed at Jack over and over again, "Leave me alone." She nearly had a nervous breakdown. She didn't want to live. The next afternoon she answered a knock on the door. A young man handed her a single talisman rose. The card read, 'All my love, till I return, El Lancelot.'

I believe Lucy is Elvis's greatest love and positively his first. They endured through his several affairs, his many indiscretions, the ups and downs of his career, and his marriage. And, of course, they endured the extremely sad and complicated life that was Lucy's. Their love for each other just might be the love story of our century. I am grateful that Lucy has shared it, and I am so sorry that they were in a situation where it had to remain a secret.

Lucy saw few fault's in Elvis. She saw many in herself. They were in love almost instantly at a time long before he became a legend….a phenomenon.

I believe that by the time you finish reading Lucy's book you will be rooting for them; Elvis and Lucy.

There's a saying, something like, 'don't criticize or speak negatively about another person's choices until you've walked in their shoes. This comes to mind because of how I feel after reading Lucy's book. My heart is filled with, 'what ifs.' In fact, 'What If' would be a great book title. Perhaps Lucy could have selected this as the title for her book. In any case, for some reason, her story has touched my heart like no other. I actually hurt for her and Elvis, and I am simply a reader. I spend way too much time thinking about their complicated love, and I try not to think about what they must have felt at times, but in the end they made it through the pain. Perhaps I am more of a romantic than I thought. I can actually feel Elvis's nervousness as he was preparing himself to make that first call to her. I can also feel the shock and the anger that Lucy felt that he had put her through such an ordeal. And I can feel the extreme joy they experienced to finally learn they could be together. It must have seemed like a lifetime, but the future would also be a lifetime. I would like to learn if Lucy is still alive. I do believe that if she is they are still together. They would never have a normal life because he had to stay un-recognized, but they had the blessing of being together and living a full and interesting life.

Lucy had a very interesting life. You will marvel reading all the shared details about this remarkable person. She endured many injustices that began when she was a mere eleven years old. And to think it was her grandmother who started it all makes me wish I could slug the old woman. But then I imagine she has paid for what she did to Lucy, so that is good enough for me.

Lucy says of Elvis, "He was strong, indomitable, and sure of himself and his beliefs. He was tender, kind, gentle, and loving. He had faults, but they were so few and small compared to his goodness." I say, "Ditto."

I encourage you to read these books. Most are out-of-print and some of the publisher's are no longer in business. I wish you luck in finding them. You can search for them as I did on Google; Amazon.com books, Alibris.com books, half.com, and eBay. I don't get involved in the auctions, but many times you can buy the book without participating in the auction.

Reading about Elvis has helped me to know and understand him. When I saw him perform on stage he always did something to amuse the audience. He made people feel comfortable. He teased the crowd. I thought perhaps it was just something he did on stage, but in the books that I have read it is clear he is downright ornery. He has an enormous sense of humor, and causes a tremendous amount of 'chuckles.' I also learned from my reading that these writers, with the exception of Patrick Lacy and Albert Goldman, truly love Elvis. I am also impressed with the women who had a relationship with Elvis.

Regardless of the unhappy and hurtful times they shared.... in the end....even though they ended the relationship they still speak of him with extreme affection; that says a lot about Elvis. I believe Elvis loved all the females that were special to him, but in his way. I believe too that he did indeed find his one true love.

One thing I have observed is that on stage he was charming, impish, and playful. This same personality comes out in the books I have read. He was simply being himself.

I am grateful for the books that I have read about this special spirit. I feel blessed and fortunate that these stories were shared. Elvis doesn't need to be angry or embarrassed that some of his 'laundry was hung out to dry.' Perhaps some of what has been written is exaggerated, and I know some of it could have been left unsaid because it was quite personal, and didn't need to be said, but I imagine the majority of what was said in what I read is correct. With his enormous amount of intelligence I hope he has learned not to sweat the small stuff. After all, he is just a man....a very special man.

Nine

It Wasn't Easy Being Elvis

I have always thought Elvis was an overnight success. It seemed that way to me because from his earliest days his talent was over-whelming, and he was received with screams of joy, but I have learned not everyone liked him.

It absolutely amazed me to learn he got some bad reviews. He had to be hurt, but after awhile he may have shrugged it off knowing, 'you can't please everyone.' And perhaps he knew it was part of 'show business.'

"Mr. Presley has no discernible singing ability."

"For the ear he is an unutterable bore."

"From watching Mr. Presley it is wholly evident that his skill lies in another direction."

"He can't sing a lick."

"Always there was something or someone, real or fictional, responsible for the imminent destruction of society as we know it. In 1956 it was Elvis and rock and roll."

"Don't give up your day job."

In some areas petitions were circulated in an effort to bar Elvis from Television. He was burned in abstention in Saint Louis and was hung in effigy in Nashville. Gads! Even Radio was not totally accepting him. One station said, "Elvis's records aren't up to station standards," so they didn't play them. A disc jockey in Nashville burned six hundred Elvis records in a public park. In Wildwood, New Jersey, a disc jockey said he could not justify playing Elvis's records. And a radio station in Uvalde, Texas auctioned its collection of Elvis records. The top bidder was an anti-Elvis group. But what did they know? I'm glad Elvis persevered and was a huge success.

His reviews changed. Perhaps it made up for some of his earlier reviews.

"Elvis is magnificent."

"In a world where meteoric careers fade like shooting stars Elvis has staying power…he is a superstar."

"Elvis remains a popular and enigmatic star."

"Elvis made a dynamic impact with just his presence."

"When Elvis performs everything about him is magic."

"His vocal ability is awesome."

It appears many of the reviewer's didn't know talent when they saw it. Elvis was different, but he was refreshing at a time when the world needed it. It was not an accident that he had an abundance of stage presence and charisma. And it was not an accident that he was gifted with a beautiful voice, a fantastic sense of whimsical humor, and a spirit full of love for all people. He was kind and generous to a fault. And he felt joyful when he put a smile on a stranger's face. Elvis must have thought his fans expected him to be perfect, so I imagine it was a bit rough for him to read the personal things written about him.

I learned he did not drink alcoholic beverages nor did he smoke cigarettes, but he liked his little cigars. Now whether he inhaled is another matter. He had quite a bad habit of swearing, and I didn't want those words penetrating my brain, but I couldn't figure out how to skip over them. Many of the guys and gals in his group had the same bad habit. Prior to 1972, I was just as bad, but it was easy for me to stop when I read that 'swearing is the way a feeble minded brain expresses itself.'

Elvis also had quite a temper. It was said in several books that he shot out several televisions'. He wasn't using them as target practice, but when someone was performing that he didn't like; bang and he replaced the TV. Will he could afford it and apparently he was not careless because there were no personal injuries…that I know of.

I developed quite a temper after I graduated from High School. I worked as a waitress at a Hotel. Something would happen to grate on a nerve, and for some unknown reason I rushed into the kitchen seething; I felt like screaming, but instead I filled a glass with water, and threw it on the floor with all the force I could muster. Every employee looked in my direction, and the waitress in the coffee shop hurried in to see what had happened. I felt better, and the bus boy cleaned up the mess I made. Not one person said anything, but they all laughed after I was out of sight. This behavior continued several times. One day I was seething in the kitchen, and just sort-of walking around in circles. The strangest thing happened. The bus boy ran up to me and handed me a glass of water. I was bewildered. He smiled and said, "Go ahead… throw it." Everyone was smiling and cheering me on. Yes! I threw it ,and it shattered. It was then I knew I had to learn to control my temper; and I did. I realized it was a very childish thing to do, and that it was wrong for me to cause another employee unnecessary work, and even though the Hotel could afford the breakage it was a destructive habit that I didn't want to continue.

So what I'm saying is Elvis surely had lots of company in the temper department and I imagine he came to terms with his temper many years ago.

Some of his moments of temper could have happened due to the influence of drugs. I was so sure he didn't do drugs, but it is clear he did abuse prescription drugs and perhaps others. It is easy for some people to get hooked on them. If a doctor prescribes them then it is easy to justify taking them even when taking a larger dose than is prescribed. In Elvis's case he did need them. He had several medical reasons that legitimately required them. His demanding schedule wrecked havoc on his body, and it became difficult to fall asleep so he began taking sleeping pills. After learning it was difficult to wake up he was prescribed a medicine that would get him going. It appears it turned into a habitual cycle.

The good thing is he is an intelligent person and he recognized he was out of control. He wanted a healthy body and a healthy lifestyle. I imagine too that he was ashamed of some of his behavior. He was strong enough to make the necessary changes required to improve his life. It required discipline, strength, and determination. I'm happy for him that he was up to the challenge.

Some of us have a better foundation than others to acquire these traits. Elvis is a work in progress just as we all are. He loves the Lord, and because of that love he had the strength to change his life for the better, and that is exactly what he did. He did it his way.

Actually he has set a good example. He is a good teacher. He has shown us that even when born into poverty we don't have to live a lifetime in poverty. He has shown us we should love each other, be kind to each other, be forgiving, and be generous regardless of the size of our bank account. I am proud of him for changing his life and hope that you are too.

I have learned his glamorous life left a lot to be desired. It wasn't easy being Elvis.

Ten

I Never Left….I Haven't Gone

Recently, a friend told me to check out a song on the internet. I don't remember where I found it, but I want to encourage you to look for it because it is a beautiful song. It was released sometime in 1988. I wish I had been able to buy a copy, but I didn't hear it until now. Perhaps it wasn't played in Anchorage or it was, and I simply didn't hear it.

It is said that Lee Stroller, the president of LS records in Madison, Tennessee was on the west coast doing fair dates with Christie Lane. When he called his office to get messages his secretary excitedly told him a limousine drove up, and four guys got out, and then a man steps out dressed in black. He was a little over six feet tall. His hair was black with a lot of grey, and he had a mustache. He put on sunglasses, and carried a small box into the office, and told the secretary, 'This is my new tape. I would like for Lee to release it on LS Records.' The secretary noticed his black leather gloves. One had an outline of a musical note, and the other a guitar. They were etched with the most beautiful diamonds she had ever seen.

When Lee returned his secretary gave him the box. He asked if the man had left his name; he hadn't. The only thing written inside the box was the title of the song; 'Spelling on the

Stone.' He quickly listened to it, and said, "Why, that sounds like Elvis Presley." It was played on several radio stations, and was immediately the first record ever in music history released without the name of the artist.

December 08, 1988 a silver Mercedes pulled into the drive at LS Records. Once again Lee was in Florida with Christie Lane. Four guys got out; all dressed in black. The fifth guy wore blue jeans, a pink shirt, and a flight jacket. With a box under his arm he walked into the office. He told the secretary he wanted to thank Lee and everybody for accepting his new song. He heard and read lots of good comments about it. In his box he had nine new songs that he wanted Lee to release. This time he wore white leather gloves with TCB etched in diamonds. When he left he simply said, "Thank you, Ma'am."

I will warn you there is more than one artist, so keep searching until you find the one that sounds like Elvis. I can share the words of 'Spelling on the Stone' with you.

People wonder, People ask, Am I present, Am I past? I never left....I haven't gone. Check the Spelling On The Stone. Was my leaving you a sin? Did my faith somehow grow thin? My secret's out....so many know. Check the Spelling on the Stone.

Chorus: Allegedly he never died. It's up to you to decide.

Say the word, and I'll come home. Check the spelling on the stone. Would you miss me quite the same had I never come to fame? So the truth may now be known. Check the spelling on the stone.

Chorus: Allegedly he never died. It's up to you (PLAY MY SONG) to decide.

Say the word, and I'll come home. Check the spelling on the stone. Just check the spelling on 'my' stone.

In the second chorus he says, "Play my song" while the girls sing the chorus. If Elvis didn't write this song, whoever did; wrote it for him.

There is much controversy about this song. In fact, I have learned there is controversy about anything regarding Elvis.

I hope that one day the masses will have the faith to believe the truth. The body of Elvis Presley did not die in 1977; and that he did say to me, with sincerity, "Don't cry darlin'."

About the author

Pepper ran away from home when she was a month shy of being fifty-two years of age. Anchorage, Alaska was home for twenty-one years. Nineteen months after she arrived in the beautiful state she had a close encounter with Elvis Presley, in a Safeway Store, around three-fifteen in the morning March 12, 1988; almost eleven years after it was reported he had died. She also shares a conversation Elvis had with an Anchorage disc jockey at radio station KYAK, October 14, 1988.

Pepper is believed to be the only writer who has published a book telling about an unexpected contact with Elvis after his reported death on August 16, 1977.

She resides in Huntsville, Alabama where her only child, Jami Lynn Dixon, lives with husband Terry Lynn. Two granddaughters; Tarah and Brittany, one grandson; Toby, and three great grandsons; Ethan, Haydn, and Noah, also live in Huntsville. Her grandson; JoShua, lives in New York City.

Since this is Pepper's first published book, and is based on a short encounter; she has read other books, and researched for more interesting information to include that Elvis fans will enjoy. Pepper hopes the reader comes away with a deeper understanding of Elvis, and why he did what he did August 16, 1977.

Contact Information

Pepper Ritter
pepperritter22@gmail.com
256-541-3122

RESOURCES AND REFERENCES

'*Elvis: A Biography,*' written by Jerry Hopkins, was published in 1972, and reprinted in 1975, by Warner Books, Inc.

'*My Life with Elvis,*' written by Becky Yancey and Clifford Linedecker, was published in 1977, by St. Martin's Press.

'*I Called Him Babe: Elvis Presley's Nurse Remembers,*' written by Marian J. Cocke, was self-published in 1979, and reprinted in 2009.

'*Elvis His Spiritual Journey,*' written by Jess Stearn, was published in 1982, by The Donning Company Publisher's. It is also published under the names of '*Elvis' Search for God,*' and '*The Truth About Elvis.*'

'*Elvis and Me,*' written by Priscilla Beaulieu Presley, was published in 1985, by The Berkley Publishing Group.

'*Elvis and Gladys,*' written by Elaine Dundy, was published in 1985, by McMillan Publishing Company, and in 2004, by University Press of Mississippi.

"*The Presley Arrangement,*' written by Monte Wayne Nicholson, was published in 1987, by Vantage Press, Inc.

'*Are You Lonesome Tonight?*' written by Lucy deBarbin and Dary Matera, was published in 1987, by Villard Books.

'Is Elvis Alive?' written by Gail Brewer Giorgio, was published in 1988 by Tudor Publishing Company.

'*Elvis, My Brother,*' written by Billy Stanley, Elvis's half brother, was published in 1989; by St. Martin's Paperbacks.

'*If I Can Dream,*' written by Larry Geller was published in 1990, by Avon Books, by arrangement with Simon and Schuster.

'The Elvis Files' written by Gail Brewer Giorgio, was published in 1994 by Shapolsky Publishers, Inc.

'*Last Train to Memphis,*' written by Peter Guralnick was published in 1994, by Back Bay Books.

'*My Love Affair with Elvis: Don't Ask Forever,*' written by Joyce Bova, as told to William Conrad Nowels, was published in 1995, by Kensington Publishing Corporation.

'*Elvis in the Twilight of Memory,*' written by June Juanico, was published in 1997, by Arcade Publishing Inc.

'*Elvis Presley's Graceland Gates,*' written by Harold Loyd, a first cousin of Elvis, was published in 1998, by Jimmy Velvet Publications.

'Elvis Undercover-Is He Alive and Coming Back?' written by Gail Brewer Giorgio, was published in 1999 by Bright Books.

The Truth About Elvis Aron Presley: In His Own Words written by Donald Hinton M.D. with "Jesse," was self-published in 2001 by American Literary Press.

'*Inside Graceland,*' written by Nancy Rooks was published in 2005, by Xlibris Corporation.

'*Return of the King: Elvis Presley's Great Comeback,*' written by Gillian G. Gaar, was published in 2010, by Jawbone Press.

'*Leaves of Elvis' Garden: The Song of His Soul,*' written by Larry Geller, was published in 2007, by Bell Rock Publishing.

What's not to love?

Elvis definitely looks like Jesse...because he is.

He now chooses to use the name of his twin brother

Elvis/Jesse Presley with his grandson, Benjamin Storm Keogh.

This picture was not intended to be shown until after his death.

However, in 2001, it was published in his book.

It's heart-warming to see him happy and healthy.

Jesse is sixty or sixty-one in this picture.

It's obvious he was taking care of himself when this picture was taken.

Check out those muscles. He is still put together real good.